Understanding
The Qur'an
A Contemporary Approach

*"To those free souls
who are seeking the truth
in the long journey of life,
I humbly present this book."*

−Mostafa Mahmoud

Understanding
The Qur'an

A Contemporary Approach

Dr. Mostafa Mahmoud

Translated from Arabic by Dr. M. M. Enani

amana publications

First Edition
(1425AH/2004AC)

© Copyright 1425AH/2004AC
amana publications
10710 Tucker Street
Beltsville, Maryland 20705-2223 USA
Tel: (301) 595-5999 / Fax: (301) 595-5888
E-mail: amana@igprinting.com
Website: www.amana-publications.com

Library of Congress Cataloging-in-Publications Data

Mahmud, Mustafa.
[Qur'an, muhawalah li-fahm 'asri lil-Qur'an. English]
Understanding the Qur'an : a contemporary approach / Mostafa Mahmoud ;
translated from Arabic by M. M. Enani.-- 1 st ed.
    p. cm.
ISBN 1-59008-022-X
1. Koran--Criticism, interpretation, etc. I. Title.

BP130.4.M289 2004
297.1'226--dc22

                                                                    2004017810

Printed in the United States of America by International Graphics
10710 Tucker Street, Beltsville, Maryland 20705-2223
Tel: (301) 595-5999 Fax: (301) 595-5888

Website: igprinting.com
E-mail: ig@igprinting.com

TABLE OF CONTENTS

Translator's Preface

This is an unusual book. It proposes to offer a contemporary understanding of the Qur'an: rather than not a different interpretation of the Qur'an, it gives a contemporary 'reading', or a view, to which today's Muslim, armed with knowledge of modem science and modem philosophy, may easily respond. Though its conclusions differ but little from those of the established exegesis, the book differs greatly in its method of approach. It makes use of recent scientific discoveries in the elucidation of many verses hitherto regarded as enigmas and unfolds certain concepts of mysticism, which make the basic principles of Islam (indeed, of any revealed religion) easier to grasp. It also contrasts, perhaps more importantly, in the manner in which Dr. Mahmoud shows the relevance of the Qur'an to the central issues of concern in today's world.

The author shows that he is genuinely trying to 'understand' the basic questions raised by the Qur'an, keeping his eye closely on the text but with his vast scientific and philosophical knowledge providing possible avenues for reinterpretation. When a 'question' defeats his best ability he simply says 'God knows' and leaves it at that. The Qur'an being a Book for all time, the author trusts in posterity to make yet another fresh approach—perhaps the future will provide our children with deeper insights into the meaning of the verses.

It is not, however, so much the answers provided as the questions asked that make this book such an interesting contribution to our thinking about Islam. It is essentially an invitation to thinking: it seeks to query rather than answer, to stimulate rather than satisfy, and, in its peculiar way, to open up new possibilities for approaching religion in a scientific age. It is bold in its challenge to the separation of religion from modem science, which appears to have started in the Seventeenth Century.

The only way of 'explaining' something satisfactorily, as Basil Willey[1] has shown is to re-express it in terms of the language (the bent of mind) of a given age. If an age is dominated by religion, religious terms must be used; if the prevalent mode is philosophic, philosophic terms must be substituted; if scientific, scientific terms. Seventeenth-Century Europe accepted science without questioning religion, for Descartes had made belief in God and the Soul axiomatic – hence their exclusion, as Spratt tells us, from the program of the Royal Society. Thinkers of the age accepted the Cartesian dichotomy (which allowed the parallel existence of science and religion) and so avoided the translation of any religious terms into the language of the nascent, but fast developing, natural sciences. There were exceptions, of course, notably the 'allegorists', but the tendency was not on the whole in favor of 'confusing' religious with scientific terms. In the Age of Reason, which now dawned on Europe, Paul Hazard tells us, concepts were re-defined (*The European Mind–The Critical Years: 1680-1715*) and vigorous attempts were made to secure the independence of science. By the end of the Eighteenth Century, with its dominant 'mechanical philosophy', religion was reduced to a vague belief in God. Every step science took in the following century seemed to widen the gap further by stressing that science and

---

1. The Seventeenth Century Background Studies in the Thought of the Age in Relation to Poetry & Religion; Routledge; (November 1986)

religion relied on two essentially different mental attitudes, reflected in their respective methods, which could never be reconciled.

When this book first appeared in Arabic, I casually browsed
through it (at a book-stand in Cairo) and my attention was
riveted to the chapter on Heaven and Hell. Here was an 'allegorist'
following in the footsteps of Grenville and echoing the dissenting
voices of the Seventeenth Century, I thought. But turning to Dr.
Mahmoud's handling of Darwinism, I realized that a more serious
attempt was being made to beard the lion. It was Darwin, no doubt,
who dealt the severest blow to religious concepts by advocating
a theory of evolution that did for many decades challenge a
central religious concept. How was Dr. Mahmoud to deal with this
'theory'? It was surely an insuperable problem, and my interest
was aroused. I wanted to know, first, whether he had recanted his
earlier views as a believer in Darwinism and, second, whether, if he
still believed in it, he could reconcile it somehow with the 'story of
creation' as told by the Qur'an. It was not, however, until I had
read the whole book that I discovered what he was doing. Rather
than relinquish his earlier positions, he now re-defined his terms,
much in the same way as the linguistic philosophers had done
(though with different results). He believes unquestioningly in, the
Qur'an's God, but does not reject the various avenues that lead to
God – Spinoza's, Russell's, Einstein's, and Jung's! The ultimate
truth about God is hidden from us and belongs in the Unseen; but
the essential truth of His existence can be apprehended in
many ways, not least of which is the 'heart' – Kant's 'inner self',
Wordsworth's 'thinking heart' or Shelley's 'feeling intellect'. The
trouble with man's thinking is that it relies too much on language;
in the few instances when man recognizes the 'sad incompetence
of human speech' his thought processes break down and

communication becomes impossible. But communication or no communication man does apprehend the truth and it does get across to other men.

In the chapter on God's Names, Dr. Mahmoud states that the fault lies in our traditional patterns of thinking, especially in our tendency to deal with the 'truth' in terms of the out-dated materialistic science of the last century. Indeed, even today physicists have, under its influence, adopted the notion that to be real a thing must be of the same nature as a piece of matter (Lange, F.A., *The History of Materialism*). Matter was conceived of as 'something lying out there in space', Professor C.E.M. Joad tells us:

> Now matter was something which one could see and touch. It followed that whatever else was real must be of the same nature as that which one could theoretically see and touch. Hence, to enquire into the nature of things we saw and touched, to analyze them into their elements and atoms, was to deal directly with reality: to apprehend values or to enjoy religious experience was to wander in a world of shadows. (*Guide to Modern Thought,* pp. 15-16)

Parallel with this view was the belief, inherited from the Eighteenth Century, that reality must be subject to the laws which operated in the physical world – that it must work, in short, like a machine. As Professor Eddington has put it, Nineteenth-Century science was disposed, as soon as it scented a piece of mechanism, to exclaim, 'Here we are getting to bedrock. This is what things should resolve themselves into. This is ultimate reality' (*Science and the Unseen World,* p. 21). The implication was, we are told, that whatever did not show itself amenable to mechanistic causation – value, for instance, or the feeling of moral obligation, or the sense of deity – was not quite real. It was a question of distinguishing what was real, 'scientific' and therefore 'acceptable' (cf. C. Cohen's Materialism Restated) from what appeared to be unreal and was thus regarded as 'unscientific' and 'unacceptable'.

Modern science has, however, challenged this whole way of thinking – and Dr. Mahmoud is well aware of this. 'Modern matter is something', Joad explains, 'infinitely attenuated and elusive; it is a heap in space time, a 'mush' of electricity, a wave of probability undulating into nothingness; frequently it turns out not to be matter at all but a projection of the consciousness of its perceiver' (ibid., p. 17). There is now no need for those who accept the results of the physical sciences to write off, as they had once to write off, as subjective illusions the promptings of the moral and aesthetic sides of their natures, and the Nineteenth-Century gulf between science and religion is in a fair way to be bridged. Indeed, there is many a modern scientist who confidently asserts that science supports religion, many a religious 'thinker' who upholds the findings of science as vindicating belief in the Unseen. The only conclusion a neutral observer – an agnostic or an atheist – may be justified in drawing is the negative one that the 'reasons which physical science was formerly thought to provide for supposing that religion was necessarily false no longer obtain, and the way is, therefore, open for a reconsideration of the religious interpretation of the universe on merits' (Joad, ibid). Such a reconsideration has been frequently undertaken with varying degrees ss of success. The point of departure also varied, and Dr. Mahmoud's early atheism has been regarded as a bold enough start; his real start was, I believe, his discovery (not re-discovery) of the Qur'an.

His beginnings as a liberal intellectual may be traced back to the late 1950's and early 1960's when his weekly articles, his

Midnight Journals, on science and philosophy, attracted large sections of the reading public in the Arab world. These were 'musings', pure and simple, never restricted by the 'systems' of the professional philosophers. Indeed, he never claimed to be one, never dabbled in epistemology, ethics or logic. A physician by training, he read avidly, roaming at will from anatomy to astronomy, from biology to zoogeography. His articles reflected the variety of the points of view adopted and the open mind with which he approached all questions of science and human thought. He was, besides, a successful author who churned out novel after novel, play after play, and relished the controversies that most of them aroused. His audience were therefore puzzled to find him change course; they had expected him to declare the inadequacy of science now that he accepted religion, but heard him uphold modem science even more vigorously, maintaining that it pointed out the road to the ultimate truth.

It has been mentioned that it was a 'spiritual crisis' that made him turn to religion; but how are we to define that term, if definable at all? One approach is to do it by negation: it was not his illness, for he had been cured long before he started his *Midnight Journals*; and it was neither 'personal' in the sense that J.S. Mill's was nor 'political' in the sense that Wordsworth's 'moral 'Crisis' was. It could only have been intellectual; but then the intellectual crises of all great philosophers that lead them back to God contain elements that are definitely nonintellectual. Whatever it was, the experience of reading the Qur'an was the light that unexpectedly drove away the shadows. The uncertainties of science melted away like morning's fog before the sure light of revelation, he tells us. The achievements of the natural sciences supported the knowledge that 'came from above'; but, being subject to perpetual alteration and modification, scientific findings confirmed the inadequacy of science as the only tool of unraveling the mysteries of existence. Man has been strenuously endeavoring to understand himself and the universe only to be baffled by the inexplicable phenomena both within and without. In fact, the more man's knowledge, the more he realizes how little he has known and the more his knowledge is called in question: new areas of the unknown seem to open up indefinitely. But it was not to conquer those areas that Dr. Mahmoud went to religion, for he admits man's need to believe in the Unknown – the Unseen. It was rather like going to nature – man's nature and God's nature; it was, he tells us, a 'natural' thing to listen to his heart and then to see what his mind had to say about it. And that was his real start.

His work has since been heuristic. His earliest steps were, of course, cautious (which is natural enough); but even after he had acquired his characteristic sure-footedness, Dr. Mahmoud's method continued to be exploratory. He says he is trying to understand the Qur'an, never claiming to have fully understood it. His style reflects his exploratory method and, with its 'obstinate questionings', has presented considerable difficulties in translation. Most formidable was the difficulty of finding a satisfactory English version for the Qur'anic verses cited in the book.

English readers must be used to hearing that it is impossible to translate the Qur'an (because it contains the words of God which are peculiar to the language in which they were revealed), though a good linguist may reproduce the meaning of the words for – the benefit of non-Arab Muslims. Consequently, scholars have shied away from the word 'translation' in favor of 'interpretation'. As commonly defined, however, 'interpretation' is confined to the conveyance of the most obvious sense, though, in Islamic studies, interpretation is the discipline of capturing the most elusive, most unobvious, senses of a given text. Muslim Interpreters have produced, still produce, different meanings of many a seemingly straightforward verse, and commentators have defended one or another of these. 'Interpretation' seems to me a no less objection- able word than 'translation', in so far as it involves a subjective element. What we are looking for in English is a word which indicates the 'reproduction of meaning' without implying that the foreign version may be regarded as equivalent or a substitute for the original. Now in the absence of such a word, and because no translator or interpreter can credibly claim to be able to produce an equivalent text in a foreign language, any word will do – translation, interpretation, rendering or what have you!

As Muslims, our freedom to 'interpret' the Qur'an is severely restricted. We are guided by the views of the Prophet's Companions and immediate successors, and the exegesis produced down the centuries by trustworthy Muslim scholars. Without such guidance any attempt at 'interpretation' will produce strange, if not wrong, results. At one time the problem of attaining the right interpretation (or the most obvious meaning) appeared to have been solved. Few scholars would disagree today on the 'surface' meaning of a given verse. But, as our understanding of our lan- guage improves and our knowledge of ourselves and the universe increases, the hidden meaning of many verses appears and, with it, the need for the interpreter and translator alike to give both obvious and hidden meanings at once. Can this be done without risking verbosity, ambiguity and even vagueness?

It has been suggested that as the Qur'an is not a Book addressed solely to the mind, the ideals of precision, economy and lucidity (highly admired in English) may be sacrificed and a language akin to the language of poetry may be used. Strange as it may seem, these very ideals are upheld by the Qur'an in every verse, though what is lucid and precise may appear enigmatic and inexplicable. True, the Qur'an occasionally resorts to the evocation of certain 'states of mind' and the translator may feel justified in using the 'language of poetry' – but which language of poetry? Doesn't this change from one age to another, from one generation to the next, even from poet to poet? May we equate the language of Milton with that of Herrick? Or, to cite contemporary examples, the language of Larkin with that of Hughes? Perhaps we can use the 'poetic devices' which all poets have used (meter, imagery, fluid syntax etc.)? But don't these again vary greatly in practice from one poet to another – to the extent that unless you are a poet yourself you will never hope to use poetic language? Doesn't a poet in a large measure make his own language?

No; poetic language, whatever our definition of it may be, will not do. Revealed in the language actually spoken by the Arabs, the Qur'an was so unique in its 'natural eloquence' that it impressed them immediately as inimitable. It is not in verse but is higher in poetic quality than anything their renowned and acknowledged poets had ever produced. And, notwithstanding the development of modern Arabic, today's reader is still struck by the uniqueness of Qur'anic expression. It is prose of a special kind: it has rhythm without being metrical; it has imagery without being poetic; and it is precise without being 'scientific' (cf. chapters 1 & 14). Qur'anic translation has not developed into a science in the way that Biblical translation has, but I trust that in the fullness of time the questions I have raised here will be dealt with by the abler minds of the linguists.

For the verses quoted, I have done my best to follow the

original text as far as possible, even whilst attempting to give the reader a feeling of the original Arabic, particularly in Chapter 1. I have relied almost totally on Arberry's excellent 'interpretation' in conjunction with Abdullah Yusuf Ali's magnificent rendering. I found Pickthall's version of the 'meaning' of the Qur'an very useful. Sometimes I had to adjust my understanding of a given verse to that of Dr. Mahmoud, sometimes my own reading differed from his and the difference was immediately pointed out paren-thetically or was absorbed in the text. I do hope I have not done violence to the meaning intended or departed from the truth; of the Qur'an God says, 'None but God knoweth its interpretation'.

As this book is not addressed to the scholar or the specialist but rather to the layman, the style I have aimed at is the 'familiar style' in Hazlitt's sense. I do not know if I have succeeded. I often found myself uncontrollably slipping into colloquial English, and I did not resist the temptation, particularly as Dr. Mahmoud's style encouraged it. Though an Arabic stylist of a very high standing, his eloquence is due not to the invariable elevation of his style but to the fact that he can vary his style to suit his audiences. In one or two chapters he departs from the familiar style to use his own brand of poetic style - elliptic, allusive and so difficult to reproduce in English. Though I did my best to avoid the stilted language of the pedants, learned words did creep in. I only hope that the media have sufficiently popularized most of them.

Perhaps a final word of, warning. Though addressed to Muslims familiar with the basic ideas of Islam, this book will be read, no doubt, by other individuals of different religions (or no religion at all) and it is to them that the following remarks are addressed. The similarities in thought and language between the Qur'an and other Holy Scriptures are only natural: Muslims recognize all God's Prophets and Apostles and are commanded by the Qur'an to regard them as belonging to ONE religion – God's.

Similarities with other religious creeds, revealed or unrevealed, are also natural. The Qur'an speaks the language of the human heart wherever humans are found and whatever the age they live in; it is a universal language rooted deep in human's natural constitution. Muslim mystics, in particular, will be found to share a good deal with mystics' of all religions, but certain differences must be stressed. Dr. Mahmoud never uses words like pantheism, panentheism or immanence because of their connotations in mystical writings (cf. J. Boehme's Six Theosophical Points, to give a prominent example). He appears at times to suggest one or more of these concepts, though a firm believer in God's transcendence, and man's free will. Determinism is rejected, except as applied to the inanimate universe: of all God's creatures man enjoys the unique freedom to disobey Him: God's will is done in the end, of course, and man is seen as an instrument of enacting it. Again, the word predestination is avoided in favor of foreknowledge; and, though they must amount to the same thing when applied to God (for God to know beforehand is to have predestined), the difference is there and it must be maintained.

Some Arabic words have been given in transliteration and their meaning (often various meanings) explained. An Arabic word may have different but distantly related etymological and idiomatic meanings and the former may thus throw light on the latter. The phonetic transcription of Arabic words may also help the reader to relate the meanings of words sharing the same 'root' but hitherto thought unrelated. The Arabic words for 'prayer' and for 'link' are *Salah* and *Silah*, respectively. The Arabic for the Day of Resurrection is *Yawm al-Qiyamah*, where *qiyamah* literally means 'rising' and is closely related, etymologically, to one of God's most beautiful names – *Qayyoum*, often translated loosely as Everlasting. But *Qayyoum* means in one context 'to whom we shall rise', in another the Overseer, from the root verb *Qama* which, when used with the preposition *ala* (over), means to oversee. In yet another context it means the Ever-Awake, as in the verse of the Chair (The Cow: 255) where it is followed by the decisive 'Slumber seizes Him not, neither sleep'; it is here an emphatic adjective derived from the same verb *qama* (to rise, to be awake).

Other Arabic words given in transliteration are those already accepted in English such as the jinn, being the plural of jinnee, and *efreet* or *ifreet* which refers to a class or category of the jinn. The common rendering of any of these as 'spirits' seems to me unsatisfactory, for the word 'spirit' must be reserved for its specific sense as the immaterial side of man, the power of immortal life breathed into man by God.

I have avoided footnotes altogether; they are interruptive and unnecessary. They often create an air of erudition or academic scholarship which would be incompatible with a book of this kind. References to the Qur'an are given immediately after the verses; but other cross-references are given in the main text.

I hope that the readers will correct and forgive my mistakes; and I take full responsibility for any flaws in the English version of this book.

Dr. M.M. Enani
Cairo, Egypt

Chapter 1

The Qur'anic Structure

My earliest memories of the Qur'an go back to my school days. A child of four, I sat in Sheik Mahmoud's Qur'anic school, among many others of my age, and looked blankly at a blackboard on which a few words were scribbled. Sheik Mahmoud moved his long pointer from one word to the next as he recited:

> By the bright forenoon
> And the brooding night;

We repeated after him, automatically, but could never understand what *forenoon* meant or why the night should be brooding. The words were repeated all the same as pleasant combinations of mysterious syllables.

My mind could be compared, at the time, to a white sheet. It was literally blank or, in an important sense, pure. I received no home education of any kind but was brought up in a family that believed in independence. Each child was free to decide what he liked and to like what he wanted. I failed my first school year, three times in a row, but nobody said anything. My exercise books bore painful witness to my family's lackadaisical attitude. A big zero adorned lesson after lesson but evoked no reaction beyond mere amusement. Asked about my performance, I often found it boring to explain how the zero came to be there or even to mention that a new zero had been won. I simply said, "The usual," and everybody laughed!

At home, no force was used to make us learned or religious; each one had his own life to live and his own responsibilities to bear. Our family differed from many other families who resorted to brainwashing and cramming the young minds with information and religious belief under threat of 'whip and stick.' The first verse of the Qur'an was therefore completely new to me. It had the same charm of novelty as arithmetic and geography. Just as the strange business of the round earth and the five continents floating about like islands in the oceans fascinated me; just as the idea that while the moon revolved about the earth and the earth about the sun they were all somehow suspended in the sky baffled me, the Qur'an too had a mysterious effect upon me. Indeed, *mysterious* is the only word capable of describing that effect. The sound of the verse quoted above still echoed within and the words haunted me. Other verses had a similar, though perhaps more inscrutable effect: they would intrude on my consciousness in the silence of the night, and I would hear my own inner voice, in the recesses of the dark, reciting:

> *Then came a man*
> *From the farthest part of the city,*
> *Scurrying...*

The verses had a force and a life of their own, as though they were independent beings. I was, of course, ignorant of the man who came from the farthest part of the city, just as I was of the bright forenoon and the brooding night. Nevertheless, the words still rang loud and the sound had a peculiar effect like an enchanted musical note. Without realizing it, young as I was, I had discovered the internal music of the Qur'anic verbal structure.

This, I believe, is one of the subtlest aspects of the Qur'anic structure. There is no end-rhyme to help the verbal pattern, nor is the Qur'an written in verse. The prose, however, is so unique that one can detect a law of verbal architecture that governs its internal musical pattern. Like other classical languages, Arabic celebrates external verbal music and Arabic poetry is remarkable for its verse rhythms. An example, in translation, may help to illustrate this:

> He questioned me, importunately,
> That maid damsel you love, so passionately,
> Is Ruby her name? Do you answer me!

The beat or the rhythm is only too obvious and is reinforced by the quality of consonants (and, indeed the vowels) which the poet is using. The division of the sentence into equal parts is equally reinforced by the cadence in each line, and the rhythm is no less reinforced by the parallel sounds within the line. All these features combine, in short, to create an air of regularity, which is easy to explain in accordance with the established science of phonetics. It is impossible to reproduce or give an approximation of the original Qur'anic sounds in translation, however, you may feel the difference between the line of verse quoted above and the Qur'anic lines:

> By the Glorious Morning Light
> And by the Night when it is still –
> Thy Guardian-Lord
> Hath not forsaken thee
> Nor is He displeased.
> (The Glorious Morning Light, 93: 1-3)

The internal music, which may be difficult to define, is a striking factor of many Qur'anic verses:

(Allah) Most Gracious
Is firmly established
On the throne (of authority).
(Ta Ha, 20: 5)

Praying: O my Lord!
Infirm indeed are my bones,
And the hair on my head
Doth glisten with grey:
But never am I unblest,
O my Lord, in my prayer.
(Mary, 19: 4)

"Verily the Hour is coming –
My design is to keep it
Hidden – for every soul
To receive its reward
By the measure of
Its endeavor.
(Ta Ha, 20: 15)

Verily he who comes
To his Lord as a sinner
(At Judgement) – for him
Is Hell; therein shall he
Neither die nor live.
(Ta Ha, 20: 74)

Each verse has its own individual musical pattern that corresponds to, if it is not governed by, the semantic structure. This peculiarity of the Qur'an has not been adequately studied, perhaps because the science of modern linguistics (and semantics) is still in its early stages. The Arabic text actually affords infinite possibilities for such studies. See how the semantic structure feeds the verbal pattern, even as adumbrated in translation:

We sent an inspiration
To Moses:"Travel by night
With My servants, and strike
A dry path for them
Through the sea, without fear
Of being overtaken (by Pharaoh)
And without (any other) fear."
(Ta Ha, 20: 77)

It is perhaps this quality that makes the Qur'an inimitable. How could anyone hope to produce verbal structures similar, even remotely, to those of the Qur'an without producing the semantic structures (i.e., the ideas) governing the internal patterns? The style of the Qur'an, so different from any pre-Islamic writing, remains impossible to imitate (notwithstanding the attempts by the enemies of Islam to cast doubt on this very quality). The fact is that as yet no human speech has been able to approximate the rhetorical brilliance of the Qur'an. Certainly, its style must have a source beyond human power. Listen to this:

Raised high above ranks (or degrees),
(He is) the Lord
Of the Throne (of authority):
By His Command doth He
Send the spirit (of inspiration)
To any of His servants
He pleases, that it may
Warn (men) of the Day
Of Mutual Meeting –
(Forgiver, 40: 15)

It is Allah Who causeth
The seed grain and the date stone to split and sprout.
He causeth the living to issue from the dead,
And He is the One to cause the dead to issue from the living.
That is Allah; then how are ye deluded away from the truth?
(The Cattle, 6: 95)

He it is that cleaveth the daybreak (from the dark):
He makes the night for rest and tranquillity
And the sun and moon for the reckoning (of time):
Such is the judgement and ordering of (Him),
The Exalted in Power, the Omniscient.
(The Cattle, 6: 96)

(Allah) knows of the tricks that deceive with the eyes,
And all that the hearts (of men) conceal.
(Forgiver/The Believer, 40: 19)

No vision can grasp Him.
But His grasp is over
All vision: He is
Above all comprehension
Yet is acquainted with all things.
(The Cattle, 6: 103)

Our Lord can reach out to the utmost
Recesses of things by His knowledge.
(The Heights, 7: 89)

Or consider the following concise verses:

He knoweth the Unseen
And that which is Open:
He is the Great, The Most High.
(The Thunder, 13: 9)

Yet these (are the men) who (dare to) dispute
About Allah, with the strength of His power (supreme).
(The Thunder, 13: 13)

Lead to:

With Him are the keys of the Unseen,
The treasures that none knoweth but He.
He knoweth whatever there is on the earth and the sea.
Not a leaf doth fall but with His knowledge:
There is not a grain in the darkness (or depths)
Of the earth, nor anything fresh or dry (green or withered),
But is (inscribed) in a Record clear (to those who can read).
(The Cattle, 6: 59)

Perhaps contributing to the uniqueness of the Qur'anic verbal structure, semantic magnitude or scale, though to be distinguished from the message of the Holy Book itself, is the quality of grandeur. Listen to the words that conclude the story of the flood:

Then the word went forth:
"O earth! swallow up thy water,
and O sky! withhold (thy rain)!"
And the water abated,
And the matter was ended.
(The Prophet Hud, 11: 44)

They are indeed, simple and straightforward words, but each laden with meanings impossible to transmit in any other verbal formula. Each has the weight of unearthly utterance: "Swallow thy waters: Abate!" – the weight of mystery, the Unseen, the unknown, the unimaginable. "It was said... It was done!" Let us quote the lines in full again:

Then the word went forth:
"O earth! swallow up thy water,
and O sky! withhold (thy rain)!"
And the water abated,
And the matter was ended.
(The Prophet Hud, 11: 44)

Can you substitute any other words and produce the same effect? Can you create the same impression, whatever your linguistic prowess be, by using the same number of words? This is, obviously, impossible, because the words, although few, are comparable only to unearthly powers. This is why the Qur'an was regarded as a linguistic miracle by the Arabs of the Sixth Century, themselves exceptionally gifted in literary expression. Even the enemies of Islam had to admit its unusual character. A professional man of letters, who never converted to Islam, Al-Waleed Ibn Al-Mugheerah, conceded as much. He, assuming Muhammad to be the author of the Qur'an, admitted:

> *By God! His words have beauty and charm; their sound fascinates, their meaning captivates; they soar so high and you could never go higher.*

Asked to defame Muhammad, Al-Mugheerah said:

> *You could say he is a magician whose words have power to make a man abandon his father's creed, to rebel against his family, and break away from his entire community.*

So, "magician" was the worst appellation that could be attributed to Muhammad by such a professed enemy. If the language of the Qur'an does not strike us today as equally fascinating, it is because we have grown too familiar with it. We have been brought up to hear the Qur'an with unresponsive ears. Our ears, equally blunted by the low, spoken Arabic dialects and colloquial written Arabic, cannot feel the grandeur of really high Arabic. Furthermore, the manner of reciting the Qur'an by professional reciters is so dull and monotonous that expressions of sorrow, joy, and warning are all given without the least variation of tone or pitch. There are professional chanters, too, who compete in setting the verses of the Qur'an to a kind of melody that hardly accords with the meaning of the words. There are occasions when the Qur'an is recited as a routine, without giving prominence to any of its features. Needless to say, the pattern of contemporary life makes man too worldly, self-involved, materialistic, and, indeed, apathetic to be conscious of the rich spirituality of the Qur'an.

I, nevertheless, believe that a man can always extricate himself from his mundane existence to recover a moment of childlike purity. Even in the midst of worldly preoccupations we can occasionally regain enough space to relish the uniqueness of the Qur'anic structure.

Listen to the way in which the Qur'an describes sexual union. A word is used which is so delicate and so gentle that it is impossible to translate. Indeed, no other language (as far as I know) could produce a similar word, not to say an exact equivalent or substitute. Here is the verse in question:

> When he enveloped her,
> She bore a light burden (unnoticed).
> (The Heights, 7: 189)

The word 'enveloped' is borrowed in Arabic from the movement of light and shade, from the mixing of colors. The night envelopes the day, and one color is said to envelop (i.e., to recede into) another. It is a word that implies the unity, even the identity that emerges in the act of love. Can a mortal mind improve on it?

There is another category of words in the Qur'an, which are so suggestive that images arise from their sound, and echoes vibrate in the imagination. Vowing by the night and day, God says:

And the Night as it dissipates;
And the Dawn as it breathes away
The darkness –
(The Folding Up, 81: 17-18)

How else could you render the quiet of the night and the quickening light of Dawn? You could almost hear the daybreak as well as see it — the twittering of the sparrow and the cock's crowing. But, if giving a warning or a threat, the words would almost explode; the verbal structure reverberates with thunderous meanings which rock its own building:

And the 'Ad – they were destroyed
By a furious Wind,
Exceedingly violent;
He made it rage against them seven nights
And eight days in succession:
So that thou couldst see
The (whole) people lying prostrate in its (path),
As if they had been roots of hollow palm trees
Tumbled down!
(The Sure Reality, 69: 6-7)

In fact, the Arabic words give us the howling of the wind, the fluttering of canvas, images of fallen palm trees, and a vast scene of desolation so succinctly that no equivalent words may be found for them in any other language. This is why the Qur'an is considered to be an untranslatable book. In Arabic it is truly the Qur'an and in any other language it is, but merely a conveying of its meaning. A verse settles it:

> We have sent it down as an Arabic Qur'an,
> In order that ye may learn wisdom.
> (Joseph [Yusuf], 12: 2)

Indeed, how can the following (given in transliteration) excel in any language other than Arabic:

> Al-Rahmanu ala al-'Arshi-stawaa
> (Ta Ha, 20: 5)

Literally, it means:

> (Allah) Most Gracious is firmly established
> On the throne (of authority)

However, the Arabic verse does not consist of the meaning of individual words, abstracted here for the purpose of convenient rendering. It consists of a whole structure of which the meaning is only a part. There is music that springs from the heart of the words, from such mysteries as are peculiar to our language — those shades of meaning that enrich the sound and are truly inscrutable.

A unique quality of the Qur'anic phrase is that it creates a sense of awe in your heart when you hear it. Not only that, but even before you have pondered its meaning, it puts the mind in the right mood to discover the hidden meanings of the verse that reinforces the initial sense of awe. The mental (more precisely, intellectual) activity, however, takes place at a later stage, which may or may not happen. A Qur'anic verse could reveal its secret to you or withhold it. You may or may not be endowed with the insight needed for the discovery of hidden meanings; however, the original sense of awe is always there. This is hardly surprising because the Author—God—is the Creator of language. The author could not have been Muhammad himself who trembled, just as any mortal would have, when the Archangel Gabriel conveyed to him God's Command: *"Read! In the name of thy Lord who has created."* Not only did he tremble and perspire heavily, but he was also unable to identify that commanding voice. Perplexed and almost in agony, he sought refuge in his wife Khadijah. He still trembled as he feared for his sanity. Khadijah, however, had kind words to say:

> *I swear by God! He will never let you down: you are charitable to your kith and kin, generous to the destitute, hospitable to your guests; you bravely bear life's burdens and vindicate the truth.*

For two long years, no verses were revealed, and Muhammad was left alone in utter perplexity, pacing the vast solitudes of the Arabian desert, wondering about that mysterious voice he had heard in the cave. If he had been a professional writer, he could have written a whole book in the interval, but he was an honest listener, pure and simple. He listened to the words of Revelation, just as you and I listen to them today, and felt the transcendental music reverberate in his soul. He was captivated by the unique phonetic structure. When the voice returned, two years later, it said:

> *O thou wrapped up (in a mantle)!*
> *Arise and deliver thy warning!*
> *(The One Wrapped Up, 74: 1-2)*

After that, verses were regularly revealed. Muhammad never pretended to be a miracle-worker. When his son Ibrahim died, a total eclipse of the sun occurred. People interpreted this as a miracle, believing that nature had shown sympathy with the Prophet, but he denied it categorically. "The sun and the moon," he said, "are two of God's signs; they are not eclipsed to mark the birth or death of an ordinary mortal." If Muhammad had been an impostor, he would have capitalized on the event and claimed that the eclipse occurred on account of his son's death. But he was truthful and honest throughout his life.

Revelation means that God revealed to Muhammad things that he had not previously known:

> *This is part of the tidings of the things unseen,*
> *Which We reveal unto thee (O Prophet!) by inspiration:*
> *Thou was not with them when they cast lots*
> *With arrows, as to which of them should be charged*
> *With the care of Mary:*
> *Nor wast thou with them*
> *When they disputed (the point).*
> *(The Family of 'Imran, 3: 44)*

> *Such are some of the stories of the Unseen,*
> *Which We have revealed unto thee;*
> *Before this, neither thou nor thy People*
> *Knew them. So persevere patiently;*
> *For the End is for those who are righteous.*
> *(The Prophet Hud, 11: 49)*

God revealed to Muhammad some of the stories of the Torah and the Gospel that had not been translated into Arabic at that time. (The first Christian text ever to be done into Arabic, the manuscript at St. Petersburg's, was not done until 1060 C.E.). The Scriptures were a Hebrew secret, confined to the Hebrews.

The Qur'an therefore challenged the Jews to produce their Book and refer to it:

Say:"Bring ye the Law
And study it,
If ye be men of truth."
(The Family of 'Imran, 3: 93)

The Qur'an also corrects some of the details in certain Torah stories. According to the Torah, Joseph's brothers traveled on donkeys, but the Qur'an has the more credible story that they used camels. This is more credible because the donkey is an urban animal, hardly capable of traveling great distances in the desert. Only camels could have taken Joseph's brothers from Palestine to Egypt. Didn't Jeremiah lament the "lying pens of the scribes" (Jeremiah 8: 8)?

The Revelation gave Muhammad information that was equally unknown to the Torah scribes and scholars. It gave him enigmatic openings to various Qur'an chapters (Surahs) such as *Ka, Ya, a, Ain, Sa'd* and *Ha Mim* which Muhammad never claimed to be able to explain. Moreover, if Muhammad were the author of the Qur'an, he would have infused it with personal feelings and reflections. But the Qur'an, as we know, is completely devoid of these. It is totally unrelated to him; if it were, it would run counter to his personal desires:

Be not in haste
With the Qur'an before
Its revelation to thee is completed, but say,
"O my Lord! advance me in knowledge."
(Ta Ha, 20: 114)

The Qur'an is therefore a transcendental reality, completely unconnected with the soul to which it was revealed; and that soul can be no more than a medium, a transmitter of a truthful report.

Numbers and letters are the subject of mystical studies. Each figure has a special significance, and each letter has a corresponding figure. Some figures are particularly hallowed, such as the figure seven. For seven are the heavens, the earths, and the colors of the spectrum, the musical notes, and the days of the week. The fetus becomes a fully grown baby in seven months, and the gates of Hell, according to the Qur'an, are seven, and the verses of the Fatihah are seven (Arabic: *al-Mathaani*, that is, the oft-repeated verses).

The letters also have secrets. In Arabic, a letter like the hard *H* (often represented in English with a dot or a dash under the *H*, but represented in the transliteration of Hebrew by a *ch*) is used in almost all words that connote heat or warmth. Note the Arabic words for *love, Hubb*; for *war, Harb*; for *fire, Hareeq*; for *pungent, Harreef*; etc. This means that the letter has a meaning in itself, significance and a peculiarity, regardless of the words in which it is used. The letter given in the opening verses of certain chapters of the Qur'an must, therefore, have a meaning in themselves. Though we do not know it, they must have certain significance; and though we cannot unravel it, their mystery is a fact: *Alif. Lam. Meem. – Ta. Seen. Meem. – Kaf. Ha. Ya. Ain . Saad. – Ha. Meem. – Ta. Say. – Qaf. – Nuun. – Say.* It is a higher study, a lofty branch of knowledge that we may not master until much later. There can be no letter in the Qur'an that is out of place or expendable; each has a specific function to perform. God is the Prime Teacher who taught with the pen, taught man that he knew not (The Blood Clot, 96:4-5). He has inspired us with the knowledge of letters and revealed to us some of their mysteries.

Of the recording and writing of testimony, God says in the Qur'an:

> Let not the scribe refuse to write:
> As Allah has taught him.
> (The Heifer, 2: 282)

In the same chapter, it is said to fear God; God teaches you. God is the real teacher. Schools and universities, libraries, and laboratories are but God's instruments of knowledge. As God has given each of us a soul capable of learning, a perceptive mind, and a retentive memory, He has provided us with the means of learning, the letters and the words, as well as the capacity for grasping their right meaning. The words for *mother* are similar in all languages, for example in Arabic, French, and English, *umm, maman, mummy,* respectively. The same phenomenon will be found to exist in languages not even distantly related (it is *muma* in the language of the African tribe of Niam-Niam). The words for *father* are also similar, Arabic *abbee, papa,* and in African languages *pupa*! Such similarities may indicate the unity of the source. We may have been inspired by a single power to use these elementary words and understand some of their implications, their secrets and uses. The fact that the letter *B* (or *P*) is used in all words for *father*, that *M* exists in those for *mother*, must imply a special quality inherent in each.

I believe that each letter has its expressive peculiarities and secrets, that only a few of these secrets have been revealed. The Qur'an gives us those enigmatic letters at the opening of some chapters as mysteries. Rather than random combinations of letters, they constitute a challenge by the Qur'an. We are promised to have an explanation later on.

Interpreters have advanced various theories concerning these letters. Some say that God views by them at the opening of the chapters; some say they constitute the most holy name of God, the secret of which He still keeps to Himself. Some have maintained that these letters are the rudimentary material out of which, God tells us, the Qur 'an has been built on. He thus, as a kind of challenge, gives us a sample of the material before showing us the complete edifice. Yet another explanation is that some of the letters constitute the names of God, e.g., *Alif. Laam. Ra. –Ha. Meem. Nuun. = Al-Rahman*, i.e., The All-Merciful.

Ibn Arabi, a famous mystic, says that they belong to a kind of divine language which the angels and the divinely instructed use in managing "cosmic affairs." In his *Al-Futohaat al-Makkiyyah* (Meccan Conquests), Ibn Arabi says that Asif bin Barchia used these letters to bring forth the throne of the Queen of Sheba to Solomon in a glance. He claims that a divinely inspired scholar, using these letters, can turn matter into energy, energy into matter, in a glance. All these are, of course, learned surmises, at best; only God knows the truth.

We are not expected to understand the whole of the Qur'an in one or two generations. The Qur'an is designed to address all times and to reveal its secrets over the entire life span of the world, so that each interpreter can win no more than a single drop of the vast ocean.

Qur'anic studies remain rewarding because the Qur'an unfolds its secrets to whomever is willing to approach it with an open mind and heart.

Chapter 2

Free Will and Predestination

Captivated by the perfection of the Qur'an's phonetic structure, which is unique in Arabic and inimitable in any other language, dead or alive, the reader becomes conscious of the divine source and his appetite is quickened. After the initial sense of awe, which elevates and purifies the soul, he becomes eager to delve deeply into the other inimitable Qur'anic structure, namely the semantic. The ideas that unfold are so rich and so profound that volumes upon volumes of interpretation may not do them justice. I shall, therefore, confine myself to a few of these ideas in the hope of presenting the Qur'anic view of some of man's eternal problems, primarily the question of freedom.

The question of man's freedom constitutes by far the most common trap of the rationalists. They are invariably heard to ask:

– If I am predestined to act as I do, why should I be taken to account for it?

– If it is God's will that things should happen the way they do, why should I be held responsible?

It is indeed a problem. Prophet Muhammad advised his companions to avoid such argument. He specifically advised, "Whenever fate is mentioned, desist from arguing." He knew, of course, that the question of fate belonged in a category of philosophic problems for which no ready solution was available in terms of the sciences of his age. He knew that such an argument should plunge them into a philosophical labyrinth wherein they would be lost. Heart-held faith was, therefore, preferable to barren, rationalistic arguments.

This advice is no longer applicable, however, as the study of philosophy is today available at most universities, and most people, even the young, can read philosophy without difficulty. The question becomes relevant, therefore, and requires an answer in philosophical and religious terms at once. This is what the Qur'an provides.

If you consider the universe — the earth, the sky, the stars, and the planets — you will realize that it is governed by a perfect order and obeys the laws of causality. Nothing that exists can disobey that perfectly established order. Armed with no more than pen and paper, you could today make calculations and establish with the utmost precision the times of sunrise and sunset, because the sun moves (apparently, at any rate) according to a fixed law. Everything around you moves in fact according to fixed laws — except you yourself! You feel, don't you, that you can do what you like!

Man is the only creature who feels he could do what he likes, that he is free and could rebel against his circumstances and even against his own nature. He is often in conflict with the world around him, perpetually engaged in a fight whose outcome nobody can predict.

Freud once made the mistake of believing in psychological determinism, according to which the human will was thought to be apparently free but really restricted by the dictates of the instincts and the mechanism of motivation. He changed his mind later on, however, concluding that instincts were no more than obscure but unshaped motives that may be controlled at will; they could be repressed, released, or sublimated. Accordingly, an instinct is today shown to be a human condition controllable by the will, just as man uses his will in controlling physical conditions. The will is therefore a fact of the human spirit that is well above man's instincts.

Let us consider another example, namely the so-called class-determinism of Marxism. According to the Marxists, class determines an individual's motives, emotions, desires, and behavior. Every individual, they tell us, acts not as an individual human being but as a representative of a class — the aristocracy, the feudalists, or the proletariat. Indeed, they deny the individual an independent soul. What he believes to be a soul is no more than a set of behavioral patterns drawn from his class. In other words, the individual is merely a medium for the perpetual conflict between social forces.

This view accounts for the severe contradictions within Marxism. How can we in the light of this view explain Tolstoy's behavior who, a feudalist, acted more like a poor peasant? An anarchist like Kropotkin provides another example. Even Marx himself, who belonged to the bourgeoisie, rebelled against his own class. On the other hand, we may come across a farmer or a worker acting against the interests of his own class. The farmer may fail to combat pests on a cooperative farm, and the worker may omit to do maintenance work on a public bus. Such determinism as postulated by class psychology is inaccurate and unscientific.

The truth is that the human spirit is unique. It differs from all forms of material existence in being able to get away from the necessary, even the inevitable. Man's will is free to violate any compact. It is impossible to predict what will happen within man's inner self insofar as this is indeed free. Nothing could prevent a man from holding something within himself. Man is the only creature who is really and truly the master of his own aspirations.

This intrinsic free will is, however, soon thwarted by the material world as man comes into contact with it in practice. A desire remains free for as long as it is latent or confined to the inner self; once it seeks concrete expression, the body obstructs it. A person's body, in fact, confines him as though it were a plastic mold. He is besieged by physical needs: he is required to provide the body with food and drink in his struggle for survival, and so he joins the rat race, and loses part of his freedom. He is the price he must pay. How otherwise can one's desires find an outlet? The body is thus a means of expressing one's freedom inasmuch as it imposes restrictions on it. Other people's bodies may also be regarded as the means of attaining our freedom; we make use of the worker's products, the farmer's produce, the writer's thought — the fruit of other people's bodies and freedoms.

Society is in effect a huge instrument for realizing our freedom. It is placed at our service with its myriad amenities – mail, transport, electricity, water supply, industry and science. When a man takes a train, he actually uses a concrete means of freedom prepared by thousands of workers, engineers, and inventors; and he has to relinquish a part of his own freedom in return for this amenity. He pays the price not only to society, but also to the world at large, in fact, even to the universe! The earth's gravity, air pressure, the oceans' water, and the stars above, all besiege him and require him to achieve a degree of harmony with them. This harmony wins him his freedom.

Harmony enables him to ride the world as if it were a horse! His knowledge about the movement of the wind enables him to put it to his service; he is now free to sail the seas! His knowledge of people helps him to live in harmony with other beings; he can serve their interests and his, winning them over really and truly, thus establishing his freedom harmoniously.

Man is therefore subject to the forces of two worlds: the world of will within, and the material world without. The latter, we know, obeys immutable, restrictive laws. His only means of freedom of action is to gain knowledge of these laws and to learn how to use them by living in harmony with them — which is always possible. Freedom is a fact. It is not negated but rather affirmed by external and adverse material conditions. Indeed, freedom becomes significant only through conflict; without conflict it is insignificant and meaningless.

Ethical codes and social laws do not negate but regulate man's freedom, serving rather like traffic lights that guarantee the freedom of passage for all. When you establish controls over your desires, you actually gain your freedom, because only then do you become the master of your fate and not the slave of your instincts.

Options of gambling, drunkenness, drug addiction, and sexual promiscuity are not freedoms at all. They are forms of suicide. They are against life and consequently against freedom. Any option against life is hardly an option at all. Any option against the law of nature is the negation of option. When we swim, we can increase our freedom by going with the current, not against it, the current being the physical laws governing our existence.

Having said that, we come to the eternal mystery of man's relation to God, and how man's freedom is related to God's will, which is absolute. The Qur'an has a few words to say on this that give us vital clues. Because the Qur'an is not a book on philosophy, it gives no more than hints that are highly revealing and significant. The Qur'an states first that it was God's will that man be free, and that man's freedom involves no coercion on either side but rather a divine will. The Qur'an states this clearly:

> *If it had been the Lord's Will,*
> *They would have all believed —*
> *All who are on earth!*
> *Wilt thou then compel mankind*
> *Against their will, to believe!*
> *(The Prophet Jonah [Yunus], 10: 99)*

Although He could do it, God wouldn't force people to believe. He wanted man to be free to opt for belief or disbelief:

> *Say: "The Truth is*
> *From your Lord":*
> *Let him who will,*
> *Believe, and let him*
> *Who will, reject (it):*
> *(The Cave, 18: 29)*

> *Let there be no compulsion*
> *In religion: Truth stands out*
> *Clear from Error:*
> *(The Heifer, 2: 256)*

> *If We had so willed, We could certainly*
> *have brought every soul its guidance:*
> *(The Prostration, 32: 13)*

> *As to the Thamud, We gave them guidance,*
> *But they preferred blindness (of heart) to guidance:*
> *(Expounded, 41: 17)*

God leaves us alone, though we prefer blindness to guidance, and His will had thus established our freedom. God actually did more. He gave us the choice whether to have any choice or not by offering us the "Trust" (that is, freedom and responsibility) which we could have declined. Man accepted, while the mountains refused, to carry the "Trust" because he was ignorant of himself and could hardly do himself justice:

> We did indeed offer the Trust to the Heavens
> And the Earth and the Mountains;
> But they refused to undertake it,
> Being afraid thereof: but man undertook it –
> He was indeed unjust and foolish –
> (The Confederates, 33: 72)

Man was ignorant of what such a Trust entailed in terms of responsibility, choice, and vanity. It entailed injustice on the part of the individual both to himself and to others. God knew of this great trial and tribulation to man, but He also knew that it would help him to be pure of heart:

> Behold, thy Lord said to the angels:
> "I will create a vicegerent on earth."
> They said: "Will Thou place therein
> One who will make mischief therein
> And shed blood? – Whilst we do celebrate
> Thy praises and glorify Thy holy (name)?"
> He said: "I know what ye know not."
> (The Heifer, 2: 30)

We do not know how God made this offer of freedom to man, that is, whether to be free or not. It could have happened at the beginning of creation (when Adam was created), or it may be a continuous process occurring at a certain level of prenatal existence. The question belongs in the "Absolute Unseen," and the Qur'an gives us no more than a glimpse.

At any rate, man has accepted the Trust, that is, his freedom that entails responsibility. Only the free can be held responsible and may be called to account for their actions. The Qur'an states this in firm and categorical verses:

> Every soul will be (held) in pledge for its deeds.
> (The One Wrapped Up, 74: 38)

> (Yet) in each individual in pledge for his deeds.
> (The Mount, 52: 21)

> Every man's fate We have fastened on his own neck:
> On the Day of Judgement We shall bring
> Out for him a scroll, which he will see spread open.
> (The Night Journey, 17: 13)

> Say: "Ye shall not be questioned as to our sins,
> Nor shall we be questioned as to what ye do."
> (Sheba, 34: 25)

> No bearer of burdens can
> Bear the burden of another.
> (The Night Journey, 17: 15)

No one may carry the sins of another; each is judged solely by his or her own work. Freedom means that man's conscience, intentions, and inner self constitute a sanctum, a holy of holies. No coercion of any kind may be exercised therein. God has pledged himself to keep it entirely free. You are absolutely free to "take action in your inner self." You can feel, think, or harbor any intentions you like. God's intervention begins only when an inner wish develops into physical action. God then would enable man to do what He had already wished or chosen to do, which is only fair, insofar as it helps to maintain harmony between inner and outer life.

> *So he who gives (in charity) and fears (Allah)*
> *And (in all sincerity) testifies to the Best –*
> *We will indeed make smooth for him*
> *The path to Bliss.*
> *But he who is a greedy miser*
> *And thinks himself self-sufficient,*
> *And gives the lie to the best –*
> *We will indeed make smooth for him*
> *The Path to Misery;*
> *(The Night, 92: 5-10)*

This is a definite promise by God to maintain harmony between action and intention; the good will be helped to do good and the bad will be left to their devils.

> *He knew what was in their hearts, and He*
> *Sent down Tranquillity to them; and He rewarded*
> *Them with a speedy Victory;*
> *(The Victory, 48: 18)*

Elsewhere God says:

> *If Allah had found in them any good,*
> *He would indeed have made them listen:*
> *(The Spoils of War, 8: 23)*

> *Then when they went wrong,*
> *Allah let their hearts go wrong.*
> *(The Battle Array, 61: 5)*

And because God has foreknowledge of everything, He speaks in the Qur'an of:

> *Those against whom the Word*
> *Has already gone forth –*
> *(The Prophet Hud, 11: 40)*

And:

> *Those for whom the Good (Record) from Us*
> *Has gone before, will be removed far therefrom.*
> *(The Prophets, 21:101)*

> *Some whom Allah guided, and some*
> *On whom error became inevitably (established).*
> *(The Bees, 16: 36)*

> *But the Word from Me will come true,*
> *"I will fill Hell with Jinns and men all together."*
> *(The Prostration, 32: 13)*

God had foreknowledge that man would do corruption in the earth, shed blood, do injustice unto himself, and that he would thus incur varying degrees of punishment. However, foreknowledge is not predestination. On the contrary, this is the only way to be fair. It is like having two apprentices – one attentive and diligent, the other rebellious and stubborn. Wouldn't you tend to encourage the first and let the second go? Your foreknowledge is not predestination, but a judgement of the character of your apprentices. Through experiencing success or failure, they would come to learn about themselves what you had already known about them.

> *(Then) shall each soul know*
> *What it hath sent forward*
> *(The Cleaving Asunder, 82: 5)*

This life is therefore more like a test field and a trial of the real mettle of souls:

> He Who created Death And Life,
> that He May try which of you is best in deed;
> (The Dominion, 67: 2)

To preclude any excuses for misdeeds on the Day of Reckoning, that is, to avert citing the influence of conventions, traditions, the environment or society as excuses for misdeeds, God says in the Qur'an:

> But there is no blame on ye if ye make
> A mistake therein:
> (What counts is)
> The intention of your hearts:
> (The Confederates, 33: 5)

and elsewhere:

> Allah will not call you to account
> For thoughtlessness in your oaths,
> But for the intention
> In your hearts,
> (The Heifer, 2: 225)

The heart is obviously the real touchstone of good works. Speaking of those who, having believed, turn away from religion, God specifies the "painful chastisement" that awaits them but again excludes some:

> Anyone who, after accepting
> Faith in Allah, utters Unbelief –
> Except under compulsion,
> His heart remaining firm in Faith ...
> (The Bees, 16: 106)

The reference is obviously to those who may be forced to say that they had turned away from belief while in their hearts they continue to believe firmly in God. It is what happens in a man's heart that counts, primarily, not outward action.

> The Day that (all) things secret will be tested.
> (The Night Star, 86: 9)

By the "things secret" are the intentions of the inner self — that region in man's soul that is free from the influence of circumstances, society, conventions, etc. It is the absolute point of departure and is free from all restraints. It is your very spirit, your individuality, which is as unique as your fingerprints. Your spirit partakes of God's own freedom in as much as it is a breath of the Lord.

> "When I have fashioned him (in due proportion)
> and breathed into him of My spirit,
> Fall ye down in obeisance unto him."
> (Al-Hijr, 15: 29)

It is because you have the Divine Essence breathed into you and are honored by enjoying free will that you are accountable for your actions. God is therefore as fair as He is generous. And, consequently, man's spirit is often associated with God's power in highly significant verses.

> When thou threwest (a handful of dust),
> it was not Thy act, but Allah's:
> (The Spoils of War, 8: 17)

You achieve victory with your own as well as God's hand; at the moment of victory your hand is identified with God's, your will with His.

An objection may be raised: Could the inner self or the intention be also predestined? The answer is a categorical "no," as the Qur'an itself explains:

> *In their hearts is a disease;*
> *And Allah has increased their disease:*
> *(The Heifer, 2: 10)*

> *Allah leaves to stray such as transgress and live in doubt.*
> *(Forgiver/The Believer, 40: 34)*

> *But to those who receive Guidance, He increases*
> *The (light of) Guidance, and bestows on them*
> *Their Piety and Restraint (from evil).*
> *(Muhammad, 47: 17)*

> *Then when they went wrong,*
> *Allah let their hearts go wrong.*
> *(The Battle Array, 61: 5)*

> *Those who behave arrogantly*
> *On the earth in defiance*
> *Of right– them will I*
> *Turn away from My Signs.*
> *(The Heights, 7: 146)*

You are free to feel, think or desire; the initiative in your inner self is entirely yours. God's intervention takes place at a later stage and accords with your intentions. He increases the disease of those who already have sickness in their hearts, but if you would be guided, God will certainly support your effort for rectitude.

God would never predestine you to harbor evil intentions or a desire to do harm to people.

> *Say: "Nay, Allah never*
> *Commands what is shameful:*

Do ye say of Allah
What ye know not?"
(The Heights, 7: 28)

The primal law of creation is for the spirit to be a holy of holies — a shrine secure from external influences. No one could force the spirit to harbor anything against man's will.

It is the great mystery, the ultimate secret of which only God has knowledge. A Prophet's tradition concerning his Companion Abu-Bakr refers to this secret.

Abu-Bakr stands better than you in the eyes of God, not
on account of his prayer and fasting, but because of a
secret harbored in his heart.

The Qur'an says:

Quite a number of the People of the Book wish they could
Turn you (people) back to infidelity after ye have believed.
(The Heifer, 2: 109)

God did not inspire them with jealousy; they are jealous of their own free will. There is a confirmation here of that region left entirely free by God within man's being. In another verse God says to Satan:

For over My servants no authority shalt thou have,
Except such as put themselves in the wrong and follow thee.
(El-Hijr, 15: 42)

This means that the devil cannot have access to your heart unless you, being perverse, allow him; he cannot force his way through. The man's heart is protected by nature, that is, by God's will; but if a person decides that his heart will be open to the devil's temptations, it will be his choice to be thus led to evil. What is in your heart is a sanctum that could never be violated; no power, however great, can force a man to change his feelings toward something or someone. You can force people to shout your name, but can you force them to love you? You can force your servant to do things for you, but can you tell how he feels about you? The Qur'an holds you to be free and to bear full responsibility for your actions, whatever the compelling physical circumstances around you.

On the Day of Reckoning we are not allowed therefore to blame someone else for our sins. We cannot say that we were forced to disbelieve, or to swerve from true religion insofar as we have within ourselves that free region, that sanctum, which no external power can conquer. And insofar as our will is free, no circumstances, however adverse, may be invoked in justification of disbelief. Referring to such adverse circumstances, the Qur'an says:

> When angels take the souls of those
> Who die in sin against their souls,
> They say: "In what (plight) were ye?"
> They reply: "Weak and oppressed
> Were we in the earth."
> They say: "Was not the Earth of Allah
> Spacious enough for you
> To move yourselves away
> (From evil)?" Such men will find their abode
> In Hell – What an evil refuge! –
> (The Women, 4: 97)

No excuses!

Having to make a choice, a man chooses what is in his inner self.

We showed him the Way:
Whether he be grateful
Or ungrateful (rests on his will.)
(Man, 76: 3)

The word *whether* clearly implies choice.

By the Soul and the proportion and order
Given to it; and its enlightenment
As to its wrong and its rights ---
(Th Sun, 91: 7-8)

This means that God has established both paths, the good and the bad, leaving the choice to man's soul. Hence the use of the conjunction "and" rather than "or," as both paths are there together and at the same time to ensure that man has a choice. The following verses confirm this reading:

Truly he succeeds that purifies it,
And he fails that corrupts it!
(The Sun, 91: 9-10)

In other words, success and failure are the responsibility of choosing self. Another verse further clarifies the point:

And shown him
The two highways?
(The City, 90: 10)

That is, God has established us on the crossroads of two highways to allow us to choose one of them. Intention is free. The inner self is free to keep whatever secrets it wants. But action is at once free and predestined.

Each one of us enjoys a degree of freedom of action. Those advocating determinism will be hard-pressed to explain the difference between the two conditions of health and disease. When healthy, the hand is free to move; when feverish, the hand shakes helplessly. Choice obtains in the case of health, necessity in the case of illness. If necessity were the absolute rule, the two cases would not be distinguishable at all. Indeed, there would be no such cases in the first place.

Freedom of action is a fact; so is destiny. The problem is to understand the nature of this duality, to see that the one does not negate the other, that fate does not negate man's freedom, or man's freedom fate. We merely infer this from verses characterized by great subtlety; it is given implicitly, rather than explicitly, so that people are not confused.

> *If (such) were Our Will,*
> *We could send down to them from the sky a Sign,*
> *To which they would bend their necks in humility.*
> *(The Poets, 26: 4)*

He could if He would, but God does not want to force us into belief so that the freedom of choice, which lies at the center of our existence, may not be adversely affected. He wants us to be free, whether we believe or disbelieve.

It was not God who made Satan a fallen angel. It was Satan who chose to be proud and vain by refusing, unlike the rest of the angels, to serve Adam.

> *(Iblis) said: "I am better than he:*
> *Thou createdst me from fire,*
> *and him Thou createdst from clay."*
> *(Saad, 38: 76)*

Satan chose vanity, unfounded in knowledge or right. Consequently, God chose him to tempt people and made his fate to accord with his will.

Similarly, God knew of the purity of Muhammad's heart and so chose him to be His Prophet.

> *And those who strive in Our (Cause) –*
> *We will certainly guide them to Our Paths;*
> *For verily Allah is with those who do right.*
> *(The Spider, 29: 69)*

It is for this reason, that is, to ensure our freedom of choice, that God hides Himself in the Gospel and hides Himself in the Qur'an. He does not want to show Himself so decisively that we would be forced to believe. He allows the Torah, the Gospel, and the Qur'an to be books in which we may or may not believe. Of the Qur'an in particular He says:

> *By it He causes many to stray,*
> *And many He leads into the right path;*
> *But He causes not to stray,*
> *Except those who forsake (the path) –*
> *(The Heifer, 2: 26)*

The verses of the Qur'an carry enough evidence, to be sure; but it is not the kind of evidence that leaves no room for reasoning and consideration. God allows you always to make your own deductions and draw your own conclusions, because He would like you to exercise your freedom. And because you are not subjected to restrictive influences, your real intentions will emerge and your work will be judged fairly.

God wants you to be, in a sense, His viceroy, His little deputy, on earth; you would pass judgment on your and other people's affairs, as a kind of test or trial.

The following verse explains how divine will and individual freedom converge, that they could never be in opposition. The 'hypocrites' had said that they would — though they actually did not want to — fight alongside the believers:

If they had intended to come out,
They would certainly have made
Some preparation therefor;
But Allah was averse to their being sent forth;
So He made them lag behind, and they were told,
"Sit ye among those who sit (inactive)."
If they had come out with you,
They would not have added to your (strength)
But only (made for) disorder,
Hurrying to and fro in your midst
And sowing sedition among you,
And there would have been
Some among you who would have listened to them.
But Allah knoweth well those who do wrong.
(The Repentance, 9: 46-47)

As their real intention was not to fight, God made them stay behind. In other words, divine will coincided with man's will. This correspondence between divine and human wills is stated more explicitly in another verse. God is addressing His Prophet:

O Prophet! say to those
Who are captives in your hands:
"If Allah findeth any good in your hearts,
He will give you something better
Than what has been taken from you,
And He will forgive you: for Allah
Is Oft-Forgiving, Most Merciful."
(The Spoils of War, 8: 70)

Divine will (fate) is always akin to the intention — which is the quintessence of choice. In the light of this we can understand why the following verses, apparently contradictory, mean the same thing in effect:

Say, "The Truth is from your Lord":
Let him who will, believe,
And let him who will, reject (it)
(The Cave, 18: 29)

But ye will not, except as Allah wills:
For Allah is full of Knowledge and Wisdom.
(Man, 76: 30)

The first verse speaks of man's free will, the second of Divine will or fate, and the apparent contradiction is resolved when we remember that God wants for man only what man wants for himself:

If anyone contends with the Messenger even after
Guidance has been plainly conveyed to him,
And follows a path other than that
Becoming to men of Faith
We shall leave him in the path he has chosen,
And land him in Hell – what an evil refuge!
(The Women, 4: 115)

God will not force a man who has opted for evil and persisted in his desire for wrongdoing to be righteous. On the contrary, God will choose for him what the individual has chosen for himself. He will make it easier for him to proceed along his chosen path so that his intentions are fully realized. Having actually done evil, the individual will be subjected to chastisement.

We shall turn him over to what he has turned to
and we shall roast him in Hell an evil homecoming

Fate here coincides with choice; there is no contradiction, as the will of God is the will of his servant. No duality!

Verily never will Allah change the condition
Of a people until they change it themselves
(With their own souls.)
(The Thunder, 13: 11)

The concurrence of both wills is only too obvious. There is the working of both at once, individual freedom and fate. Man takes action of his own free will, while God in fact wills it to happen; for both must concur. Your capacity for choice is God's gift; it is a divine will. Your freedom is divine will; hence the verse:

But ye will not, except as Allah Wills:
For Allah is full of Knowledge and Wisdom.
(Man, 76: 30)

Far from being a paradox, therefore, this is a simple statement of fact.

But Allah was to bring forth what ye did hide.
(The Heifer, 2: 72)

God brings forth whatever is hidden in one's heart so that each one would have his own intentions materialized. Each would bear responsibility for his actions insofar as it is based on free choice. A decisive verse settles the question once and for all:

And know that Allah cometh in between a man and his heart,
And that it is He to whom ye shall (all) be gathered.
(The Spoils of War, 8: 24)

This means that God leaves the heart quite free, so that each individual will have a free inner self; God only exercises His power between a man and his heart. In other words, God sometimes prevents man from wrongdoing even though a man wants it. God never intervenes at the level of thought, feeling, or intention, but He may intervene at a later stage and then only at the level of action. As has been mentioned, the action encouraged and facilitated by God is normally of the same nature as the intention. But sometimes the heart is wayward; and God may desire to protect a good man from the vagaries of the heart and He therefore intervenes to help His good servant.

> Remember in thy dream Allah showed them to thee
> As few: if He had shown them to thee as many,
> Ye would surely have been discouraged, and ye would
> Surely would have disputed in (your) decision:
> But Allah saved (you) for He knoweth
> Well the (secrets) of (all) hearts.
> (The Spoils of War, 8: 43)

This is an instance of unobtrusive divine intervention. God wants to urge Muslims to fight the battle at Badr even though they are outnumbered (they were only three hundred facing a thousand-strong, better equipped army). He wants the Muslims to fight of their own free will, and so He reveals to the Prophet, in a vision, that his enemies are few and hardly invincible. On the battlefield God reinforces this feeling while encouraging the infidels to believe that the Muslims can easily be defeated. He thus makes both sides fight a battle the result of which He had previously determined.

A kind of preordination, no doubt; but then it accords with the free will of each party. And it is the will, deep down in the recesses of our inner selves, for which we are responsible.

These Qur'anic verses, gleaming like secret fountains of light, provide the key to the apparently insuperable problem of choice and preordination — a problem which man's philosophic approach has found to be a hard nut to crack.

Chapter 3

The Story of Creation

The beginning, Creation. How did it happen? The birth of the earth, the moon, the sun, and the stars, How did it all happen? How did the first man step on this earth? From where did he come? All these are questions which have been handled under various disciplines – biology, anthropology, astronomy, organic chemistry, geology, evolution (now an independent science), genetics, and anatomy – in volume upon volume of scientific material and with a variety of evidence and theories being advanced in support of one view or another. We cannot simply ignore all this as we read what the Qur'an has to say about Creation. Islam has never been isolated from life or opposed to science, because Islam provides us with ultimate knowledge — facts that are certain as distinguished from the myriad possibilities and probabilities of science. Islam gives us the final word and, consequently, we cannot discuss it without really discussing everything else – without, that is, discussing the question from the scientific, religious, philosophical and political points of view.

I have actually dealt with the subject rather fully in two books published in Arabic some time ago, *The Mystery of Death* and *The Mystery of Life*. I shall not, therefore, repeat what I already said in them. I believe I may, however, sum up my central argument in a general way. Let me begin by outlining Darwin's vision of the evolution of life, a vision that has changed man's thinking about himself and the world.

In a voyage around the world aboard his ship, *The Beagle*, Darwin managed to marshal certain data about all living things on land, in the sea, and on the seabed. He established the following observations:

– Living creatures continually change and adapt themselves to their environment.

– Man in the arctic zone is fat, just like whales, as though the extra layers of fat were meant to protect him from the cold. In equatorial zones man is lean and black, as though the dark color was meant to protect him from the sun.

– Cave lizards which live in the dark have no use for physical vision or skin color; they are consequently blind and uncolored. Prairie lizards are, on the other hand, sharp-sighted and colored.

– Animals' mouths vary according to function. There are mouths equipped with dagger-shaped teeth which cut and tear the flesh, like a tiger's mouth; a mouth equipped with a beak, like a bird's; another with a hose for sucking blood, like a fly's; another with a needle, like a mosquito's; and others with saws and grindstones, like insects'.

Should we assume that all animals share a common origin which, developed in various ways to produce a wide variety of species dictated by the different environments on earth? Animals living on land developed legs; those in the sea had their legs developed into fins, while those who fly had their arms developed into wings? If such an assumption is correct, all animals must have similar physical structures. And this the lancet confirms. A snake, which has no legs, has been found to have atrophied limbs hidden within its skeleton. Birds which appear to have only one pair of limbs have been shown to have another pair developed into wings to suit the newly acquired function of flying. Fish that today live on land (amphibiously) have been proven, anatomically, to have lungs developed from ancient 'float bladders'. The four fins are oar-like appendages developed from the old limbs. Fingers and toes are always five: in man, apes, mice, lizards, and even in bats, though they are atrophied here. The heart and blood circulation are the same in whales, mice, apes, man, and bats; the same arteries are to be found in each species, and the heart is the same with its four chambers. The nervous system, which consists of a brain and sinews, etc., is the same in each. The muscular system and the skeleton are similar, with a few modifications necessitated by different functions. The same genitals, testicles, ovaries, uterus, etc., are to be found in every animal. Pregnancy in humans lasts nine months, as it does in the primates and other mammals (whales, for instance); and all nurse their young for two years.

Another discovery: human anatomy shows the tail vertebrae of the apes, though again atrophied and stuck together, as having no function to perform; the tail muscles have developed into a solid support for the pelvis. There are seven vertebrae in the human neck, the giraffe's neck and the hedgehog's!

It was further discovered that an embryo evolves in phases in the uterus. At one stage it looks like a fish with fins; at another it develops a tail which gradually disappears; at a third it becomes completely hairy, but then the hair recedes leaving a limited hairy area on the head. It was the embryo that told the whole story – the story of the beginning, and the stages of evolution.

Tampering with man's ear, the lancet has made yet another discovery: behind the ear are the ear muscles that had moved the ears of man in the past, in much the same way as donkey's ears move today. The human ear muscles are again atrophied because our ears have taken their present shape and position and so deprived their muscles of all functions.

Fossils have given us human skulls close in shape to those of apes, in Transvaal, Peking, Java, and Neanderthal. Some of these skulls were discovered in caves where the relics of charred wood in primitive stoves show that those early men had known fire and used it millions of years ago.

With this evidence in hand, all Darwin had to do was to sit down and formulate his theory of the "origin of the species." Indeed, the theory seemed to require hardly any "formulation." It was there: all species evolved from the same origin; the root produced a tree with various branches, and genus and species varied according to varying environments.

Darwin does not say that man evolved from the ape or that the human race evolved from chimpanzees or monkeys. This is merely a joke popularized by the press and spread about as a humorous caricature of Darwinism.

As formulated by Darwin, the theory does not say that any of the existing species evolved from any other species, however anatomically similar, but that each is an independent branch of the tree of life. No branch sprouted from another (nor is the human branch a variety of the ape branch) but each emerged independently from the parent tree and both can be traced back to the same source, namely the initial living cell. It is the cell that constitutes the nucleus of every living organism, each varying according to various environments. No species evolved from another, but each is the apex of its particular genus and is independent enough in constitution to be incapable of producing another branch, another species.

Darwin thoroughly examined evolution as a natural

phenomenon. What he says about adaptation between a given creature and its environment explains nothing beyond congenital and functional differences between creatures; it cannot explain their evolution from the low to the high. An explanation had to be found. Darwin ventured a new idea, namely that evolution was due to purely "internal" reasons, that is to say, without a guiding hand from outside. The struggle for survival was the sieve through which the fittest passed. Breeding and inter-breeding produced different combinations with varying degrees of fitness. A "new combination" whose feet were equipped with flaps proved fitter to life in water and therefore survived at sea: all other water "beings" who lacked flaps could not survive. "Survival for the fittest" came to be a dictum too attractive to resist; and the concept of evolution was, as a natural corollary, solely based on the idea of physical, biological forces. In the light of this, living beings underwent a forced or inevitable process of evolution that, however, appeared spontaneous enough.

In the following years the "theory" was tested and re-tested at the largest scale possible. A number of its essential doctrines survived, but many others were rejected. That all species had evolved from a single parent source but were differentiated later on under the influence of the environment appeared a plausible conclusion. It was likely to be correct in view of the evidence available: family ties existed between different creatures and they all seem to be related anatomically to one another. But the assumption that such evolution had taken place by force of purely biological necessity, that is, without a guiding hand, was no longer convincing.

Indeed, why should an animal like the horse evolve from the ass when the latter is more sturdy and robust? What material forces could prompt the evolution of the gazelle out of the antelope when the former is hardly as tough or strong as the latter? Consider the delicate, colorful butterflies which are slower and more fragile than the humming tough-looking wasp; or the pigeons, palm-doves, peacocks, and budgerigars which are more delicate than hawks, kites and vultures. The evolution of these species cannot be explained in terms of "survival for the fittest" but rather in terms of "survival for the most beautiful."

"But most beautiful according to whom?" a sly critic will ask, "Surely beauty is in the eye of the beholder," and is beauty in the animal kingdom determined by the laws of procreation? A female bird is attracted to the more colorful bird for the purpose of reproduction; "natural selection" is at work here too. The determining factors are purely material and biological!

This view is, however, most untenable and can be easily refuted. Why should a female choose a more beautiful male? A spotted colored wing is not fitter for flying than a plain one, and biological interests are hardly at stake here. Rather we have high aesthetic values that outweigh all other forces. Here is the mind of the creative Artist turning out beautiful creatures. We see His touch in tree leaves, the colors of flowers, the wings of butterflies and peacock feathers.

We wonder at some desert plants that have winged seeds that fly for miles over arid land in search of water. We wonder at mosquito eggs that are provided with airbags to help them stay afloat. This cannot be explained except in terms of the Universal Mind: the Greater Mind that thinks for His creatures. For neither the desert plant nor the mosquito possesses a mind. The plant cannot supply its seeds with wings, and the mosquito cannot supply its eggs with airbags. These are natural phenomena that cannot be explained in terms of Darwin's theory, but only in terms of the Universal Mind that plans and creates all beings.

To illustrate this point, let us take a hypothetical example. Let us assume, for the sake of argument, that our vision is so flawed that our eyes can only see the machine but not the maker of machines. We may, then, see the handcart, the horse-cart, the hackney, the motorcar, the steam locomotive, the diesel-fueled engine, and the electric train, but not man. We should say that these things evolved from one another by stages. We should try to prove our point with reference to their anatomical similarities. They are all made of wood, iron, and leather, and their bodies are drawn on wheels. Indeed, anatomy, a respected science, tells us that these bodies share the same components and move in the same manner, notwithstanding their different fuels – steam, petrol or diesel.

Because we cannot see the maker, we should assume that they have come to acquire their different shapes as a result of evolution, impelled by internal factors, as a result of a long struggle for survival in various environments and having passed through the "survival for the fittest" sieve. We shall deny the existence of the outside factor because we cannot see "him" and because we can see that they are all motored by an internal engine.

The mistake that Darwin made in formulating his evolutionary theory was to claim that evolutionary factors were purely internal. To put it differently, he made the mistake of denying the guiding hand of God simply because he could not see it. We thus have a theory that reveals family ties among living beings but does not explain how evolution takes place.

As to what science tells us about the beginning of life, we have a consensus of opinion that life started in water, perhaps in swamps where matter fermented, so that by a myriad process of analysis and synthesis (controlled by mysterious forces), the very elementary substance of all living things, protoplasm, came into being. Nobody knows exactly how this happened but, at a wild guess, we could attribute it to a combination of water and earth.

Regarding the beginning – the stars, planets, and interstellar bodies– astronomers are in agreement that the universe had its origins in gas clouds and nebulae of particles of dust. The condensation of such clouds was caused, it is believed, by the force of gravity, and the result was a kind of atomic structure where there was a nucleus in the middle (the sun) and lesser and dimmer bodies orbiting it (the planets). Each solar system has this typical structure, and in each galaxy there may be hundreds, even thousands, of such systems.

This is how much science has contributed to our knowledge of the story of creation. What did the Qur'an say about this fourteen centuries ago? What did the Prophet say, when neither he nor his people had heard of biology, geology, organic chemistry, genetics, anatomy or anthropology?

The Qur'an has its distinctive style. When it deals with a scientific question, it does not present it in terms of equations, as a mathematician would, or in terms of its anatomical details, as a biologist might, but it uses oblique terms, symbols, figures, metaphors, swift-shifting suggestions and expressions which shine like lightning in our minds. It puts in a word here, and another there, which may be impossible to interpret immediately. God knows, however, that a time will come when man will understand.

Soon will We show them
Our Signs in the (furthest)
Regions (of the earth), and
In their own souls, until
It becomes manifest to them
That this is the Truth.
Is it not enough that
Thy Lord doth witness
All things?
(Expounded, 41: 53)

About the Qur'an, God says:

But no one knows
Its true meanings except Allah
(The Family of 'Imran, 3: 7)

Nay more, it is
For us to explain it
(And make it clear)
(The Resurrection, 75: 19)

These passages mean that God will explain the Qur'an to us in the fullness of time. Has that time arrived as yet? Let us try at any rate to find out what the Qur'an has to say about the story of creation. Of God, in the very beginning, it says:

Moreover, He Comprehended
In His design the sky,
And it had been (as) smoke
(Expounded, 41: 11)

So in the beginning something like smoke had existed and from this the universe was created.

He created the heavens and the earth
In true (proportions):
He makes the Night overlap the Day,
And the Day overlap the Night
(Crowds, 39: 5)

This verse is difficult to interpret unless we assume the earth to be spherical and the night and day being the two halves of the sphere sliding into one another as a result of its continuous revolution. Indeed, the use of the verb "overlap" transitively in this context is quite unusual; but it forces on us the interpretation just given.

And the moon – for which –
We have determined phases (which it must traverse)
Till it becomes like an old date-stalk, dried up and curved.
(Yaseen, 36: 39)

The aged palm-bough is dry and lifeless – an apt simile for the moon that lacks water and vegetation and is quite lifeless, but shaped like a sickle in the new moon phase.

Neither may the sun overtake the moon
Nor can the night outstrip the time of the day
Since all of them float through
The orbits of space (in accordance with Our law).
(Yaseen, 36: 40)

Indeed, the Qur'an describes space with its paths and orbits in the following tidy description:

By the sky with (its) numerous paths
(The Winds that Scatter, 51: 7)

The Qur'an refers to a recently discovered scientific fact, namely that behind the apparent stillness there is motion within, even in the substance of apparently dead matter:

> And thou wilt see the mountains,
> Which (now) thou deemest so firm
> Pass away as clouds pass away:
> A work of God, who has ordered
> All things to perfection.
> (The Ants, 27: 88)

The comparison with clouds is particularly significant. It suggests loose atomic structure, which is actually correct; "solidity" is a mere illusion, and each seemingly solid object consists of atoms in a state of flux; indeed, the entire planet Earth is in a state of perpetual motion.

Early Qur'anic commentators believe that this verse refers to what happens on the Day of Resurrection, but they are wrong. The Day of Resurrection is a day of certainty when there will be no room for speculation or doubt. What happens to the mountains on that day is stated elsewhere in the Qur'an:

> And they will ask thee about (what will happen to)
> The Mountains (when this world comes to an end)
> Say, then: "My Lord will unlevel them
> And scatter them far and wide.
> And leave the earth level and bare."
> (Ta Ha, 20: 105)

Such is the Day of Resurrection: there will be no chance of pondering what the mountains are like because they would have been scattered to ashes. The former verse must therefore refer to the mountains in this world.

The Qur'an also tells us what happens to rain water:

Seest thou not that Allah
Sends down rain from
The sky, and leads it
Through springs in the earth?
(Crowds, 39: 21)

This explains the cycle of ground water: it comes down first from the sky, runs on the surface of the earth, goes underground into natural reservoirs then, gushing out in fountains and springs, goes back to the earth's surface. A direct reference to life occurs elsewhere:

We made from water every living thing
(The Prophets, 21: 30)

And Allah has created every animal from water
(The Light, 24: 45)

"Does thou deny Him who created thee out of the dust,
then out of a sperm-drop, then fashioned thee into a man?"
(The Cave, 18: 37)

Behold! thy Lord said to the angels:
I am about to create man, from sounding clay
from mud moulded into shape
(Al Hijr, 15: 28)

The "mud molded" refers to an organic process of fermentation, so the Qur'an says first that life is created out of water, then that it is created of dust, then of clay, that is, of a mixture of dust and water in a state of fermentation. It is precisely what science has come to tell us fourteen hundred years later. Elsewhere the Qur'an gives more details of the creation of man:

It is We Who created you
And gave you shape;
Then We bade the angels
Bow down to Adam, and they
Bowed down; not so Iblis;
He refused to be of those
Who bow down.
(The Heights, 7: 11)

The verse establishes the fact that man was created in stages – the operative word being "then," which refers to a period of time elapsing between the first creation and the final shape given to man. Time in the Qur'an is not measured by the worldly divisions of days and weeks.

A day in the sight of thy Lord
Is like a thousand years of your reckoning
(The Pilgrimage, 22: 47)

The angels and the Spirit ascend unto Him in a Day
The measure whereof is (as) fifty thousand years.
(The Ways of Ascent, 70: 4)

Such is the measure of God's days: they are more like whole eras or ages by our reckoning. So when God says, "We created you, then we shaped you," with the culmination occurring in Adam's creation "then we said to the angels: 'bow yourselves to Adam', " the implication must be that Adam was the result of a lengthy process of creating, shaping, and perfecting which might have taken millions of earthly years or a few of God's days.

The Qur'an offers an explicit statement that man was created in stages.

"What is the matter with you,
That ye place not your hope
For kindness and long-suffering in Allah –
Seeing that it is He that has created you
In diverse stages?"
(The Prophet Noah, 71: 13-14)

Consider the following:

Has there not been over man a long period
Of Time, when he was nothing – (not even) mentioned?
(Man, 76: 1)

He said: "Our Lord is He who gave to each
(Created) thing its form and nature,
And further, gave (it) guidance."
(Ta Ha, 20: 50)

This means that God guided the process of creation until it reached its apex in Adam.

There is not an animal (that lives) on the earth
Not a being that flies on its wings,
But (forms part of) communities like you.
(The Cattle, 6: 38)

And Allah has produced
You from the earth
Growing (gradually)
(The Prophet Noah, 71: 17)

The first verse establishes close links between the human race and the other 'nations' of the animal kingdom; the second extends the relationship to cover all living things—men, animals, and plants.

Man We did create from a quintessence (of clay)
(The Believers, 23: 12)

This is a direct statement. It explicitly says that man was not created in the beginning out of clay but rather out of a certain breed developed from clay. There is, therefore, an intermediate stage between clay and man – a stage of various successive breeds culminating in the superior breed of mankind.

Of the formation of the human fetus the Qur'an tells us that bones are created before the muscles:

> *clothed the bones with flesh*
> *(The Believers, 23: 14)*

Embryology tells us that the backbone is created before the formation of the muscles. The Qur'an says:

> *He it is Who shapes you*
> *In the wombs as He pleases*
> *(The Family of 'Imran, 3: 6)*

Creation in the uterus is done in stages – creation after creation. The threefold shadows are the darkness of the abdomen, the darkness of the uterus and, lastly, the darkness of the amniotic membrane; that is, we have a chamber within a chamber until we reach the fetus. These are anatomical facts. The threefold shadows could alternatively be the three membranes of the fetus – another anatomical fact.

> *That He did create in pairs – male and female*
> *From a sperm drop when lodged (in its place)*
> *(The Star, 53: 45-46)*

We know now that it is the sperm, not the ovum, that determines the sex of the fetus.

How did the Qur'an arrive at these conclusions that are in complete accord with the conclusions of modern science? A coincidence? Granting that one is a coincidence, can we believe that all others are also "coincidences"?

How can the mind of an unlettered prophet arrive at the answers for so many questions that were completely unknown in his age but which have been proven correct more than thirteen hundred years after his death? To accept the Western atheist explanation that the words uttered by Muhammad represent the activity of an inner mind to which was revealed the ultimate truth is to admit politely and scientifically the existence of revelation. Indeed, the ultimate and absolute truth cannot be but God, and to be able to hold communion with Him is to be divinely inspired.

The story does not end here, however, as the Qur'an proceeds to tell us more than science does. The Qur'an tells us what happened in the Unseen – all that had happened in the Higher Assembly in the Kingdom of God. We are told that when Adam was created, God put him in the Garden, that is, the Garden of Paradise, wherein he was allowed to eat the fruits of all trees except one. We are told how God made the angels to bow themselves down to Adam, which all of them did.

> they bowed down except Iblis.
> He was one of the jinns and he
> Broke the Command of his Lord.
> (The Cave, 18: 50)

In disobeying the Divine Command, Satan had this to say:

> (Iblis) said: "I am better than he: Thou createdst
> Me from fire, and him Thou createdst from clay."
> (Saad, 38: 76)

He could not fathom God's purpose in honoring a creature of clay. God knew, however, that Adam would undergo great suffering as a result of being thus created – of both clay and spirit. Man would be torn apart by the conflict between the low desires of his body and the highest desires of his soul.

> Verily We have created
> Man into toil and struggle.
> (The City, 90: 4)

The trouble is nothing more than the conflict inherent in every human being between the two sides of his nature, which is designed to earn him a higher position than that of both the jinn and the angels. This is the symbolic significance of God's command to the angels to bow down to Adam. Proud and exultant and conscious of the superior substance of which he was created before Adam, Satan would not bow down to the new creation.

> And the jinn race, We had created before,
> From the fire of a scorching wind.
> (Al Hijr, 15: 27)

Fire pure means either intensely burning or pure fire. Now that Satan had incurred God's wrath, he had to be deprived of the bliss of being close to God. Rather than repent and redeem his sin, Satan completely despaired of forgiveness. This was his second sin. He, therefore, swore vengeance, pitting his wits against Adam's "humanity," and vowing to do him harm insofar as Adam, Satan thought, was the reason for his removal from Heaven. And this was his third sin. The devil had, therefore, tried to redeem a sin by committing another and consequently continued to sink lower and lower still.

Satan then tempted Adam to eat the fruit of the forbidden tree. He whispered to him that it was the tree of immortality, when it was in fact the tree of mortality.

Thus did Adam disobey His Lord,
And allow himself to be seduced.
(Ta Ha, 20: 121)

God granted Adam freedom by breathing His Spirit into him. He gave him the choice whether to be governed by His immutable laws, just like the stars in their orbits, or to have freedom and responsibility by carrying the Trust.

We did indeed offer the Trust
To the Heavens and the Earth and the Mountains
But they refused to undertake it.
(The Confederates, 33: 72)

Man did not realize the risks involved in carrying that Trust. He foolishly accepted it because it implied freedom. But God knew what it entailed, that man could only hope to avert these risks by obeying God and avoiding the forbidden tree. Only thus could he be assured of the Garden – the Paradise of obedience and submission to the Law of God.

Man had, however, chosen to be free and responsible. Upon being tempted by Satan, he disobeyed God and ate from the forbidden tree. He was now accountable for his actions and stood to deserve punishment. His punishment consisted in being deprived of Paradise and in falling down to the world of toil and labor.

The difference between the sins of Adam and Satan was that Adam went back to God, repenting, hopeful of His forgiveness, while Satan persisted in disobedience and despaired of God's mercy.

Then learnt Adam from his Lord words of inspiration
And his Lord turned towards him;
For He is Oft-Returning, Most Merciful.
(The Heifer, 2: 37)

God granted Adam mercy and promised to give guidance to his seed. He established man on earth wherein he would rule by power of will and reason as God's viceroy:

> *Behold, thy Lord said to the angels:*
> *"I will create a vicegerent on earth."*
> *They said: "Wilt Thou place therein one who will make*
> *Mischief therein and shed blood? –*
> *Whilst we do celebrate Thy praises*
> *And glorify Thy holy (name)?"*
> *He said: "I know what ye know not."*
> *(The Heifer, 2: 30)*

The angels said this because they had seen that Adam was created in stages from animal ancestors that had shed one another's blood and fought each other perpetually. Their knowledge must come from past experience because only God is capable of foreknowledge. Their objection was, as it were, overruled when God said,

> *"I know what ye know not."*

Man has earned a higher position than the angels, God knew, owing to the peculiar circumstances of his rise and the conflict ingrained in his nature between clay and spirit. He had acquired, over a long period of time, certain abilities which qualified him to be God's viceroy on the earth – a fact that God reveals now to the angels:

> *And He taught Adam the names*
> *Of all things; then He placed them*
> *Before the angels, and said: "Tell Me*
> *The names of these if ye are right."*
> *They said: "Glory to Thee: of knowledge*
> *We have none, save what Thou*

Hast taught us. In truth it is Thou
Who art perfect in knowledge and wisdom."
He said: "O Adam! tell them
Their names." When he had told them,
Allah said: "Did I not tell you
That I know the secrets of heaven
And earth, and I know what ye reveal
And what ye conceal?"
(The Heifer, 2: 31-33)

There was he! Earthly Adam possessed of qualities higher than those of the angels. This implies that God had made Adam his first prophet on earth. The fact that he was taught the names, all of them, means that he now received divine inspiration.

Another significant fact revealed by this verse is that the human mind is only qualified to learn the names of things, not their essence. Man's capacity for learning is restricted because the mind can only grasp the outer limits, quantities, and relations but never the essence of things. This has been shown repeatedly by modern philosophers.

God is referred to in the Qur'an as *Rabb* which means "master" (cf. Hebrew *Rabbi* = my master) – a teacher, a shepherd, a guide, a kind and merciful Lord who takes care of His creatures and provides them with means of livelihood.

God promised Adam that He would appoint prophets to guide Adam's seed:

We said: Get ye down all from here:
And if, as is sure, there comes to you
Guidance from Me, whosoever follows
My guidance, on them shall be no fear,
Nor shall they grieve.
(The Heifer, 2: 38)

The Qur'an explains the meaning of following God's guidance. Man can be guided to understand his mistake and may, therefore, strive to regain the Paradise lost by his father – the Paradise of obedience and submission to God's laws. This is the return to God to which the Qur'an frequently refers. Man should realize that he owns nothing except his inner self or conscience (the sanctum or holy of holies which God leaves free) and that he should submit it to God and God's laws of his own free will. Only thus could he prove better than the world of inanimate objects that submit to God's laws forcibly – from the pebble on the roadside to the stars in their orbits. Man submits willingly and out of love for the dear God who made us all. In doing this, however, man should understand that God's will must be done whether man likes it or not, and that God alone controls everything, that He alone can guide him because of His knowledge and power.

There are other abstruse verses in the Qur'an which imply that we, Adam's seed, had a previous life to this one on earth:

When We shook the Mount
Over them, as if it had been
A canopy, and they thought
It was going to fall on them
(We said): "Hold firmly
To what We have given you,
And bring (ever) to remembrance
What is therein;
Perchance ye may fear Allah."
When thy Lord drew forth
From the Children of Adam
From their loins –
Their descendants, and made them
Testify concerning themselves, (saying):

"Am I not your Lord
(Who cherishes and sustains you)?"—
They said: "Yea! We do testify!"
(This), lest Ye should say on the Day
Of Judgement: "Of this we
Were never mindful."
Or lest ye should say:
"Our fathers before us
May have taken false gods,
But we are (their) descendants
After them: wilt Thou then
Destroy us because of the deeds
Of men who were futile?"
Thus do We explain
The Signs in detail;
And perchance they may turn (Unto Us).
(The Heights, 7: 172-174)

It is a strange incident that God relates in this verse. The implication is that we had existed in God's world before we came down into our mothers' wombs (perhaps in the world of ideas of the Divine Kingdom, and possibly as spirits – no one knows.) The verse further implies that God made us testify to His Godhead and took a compact with us to that testimony so that we would not relapse into infidelity claiming to have been victims of our fathers' ignorance. We come across more references to this 'compact' in equally abstruse verses:

Behold! Allah took
The Covenant of the Prophets,
Saying:"I give you
A Book and Wisdom;
Then comes to you

A Messenger, confirming
What is with you;
Do you believe in him
And render him help."
Allah said: "Do ye agree,
And take this My Covenant
As binding on you?"
They said: "We agree."
He said: "Then bear witness,
And I am with you
Among the witnesses."
(The Family of 'Imran, 3: 81)

Here are the Prophets assembled for God's compact, namely to support one another. How did it happen? Where? When?

Such verses as these are highly significant insofar as they reveal mysteries by oblique expression. We had a spiritual, prenatal existence somewhere with God; we had existed before birth and will continue to exist after death.

Among God's names are the Creator, the Maker, and the Shaper. The Creator is He who creates us as spirits. The Maker is He who determines (allows) our existence just as a king makes someone a knight or an important functionary. The Shaper is He who shapes our material molds in our mothers' wombs. A tradition of Prophet Muhammad refers to such prenatal existence: "I was a Prophet when Adam was still unshaped clay." God tells Muhammad in the Qur'an:

Say: "Truly, my prayer
And my service of sacrifice,
My life and my death,
Are (all) for Allah,

The Cherisher of the Worlds;
No partner hath He
This I am commanded,
And I am the first of those
Who bow to His Will."
(The Cattle, 6: 162-163)

This implies that Muhammad had existed before all prophets, inasmuch as the Qur'an regards all prophets as Muslims. The more relevant implication for us is that man's spirit had existed prenatally; it had lived with God before coming down to the womb.

Going back to that forbidden tree, we should enquire whether it is a real or a metaphoric one. A good deal of controversy has arisen over this. Some commentators believe the tree to be a symbol of knowledge but then it is most unlikely that God had forbidden man to eat of the tree of knowledge. I find this explanation incompatible with God's command to man to acquire knowledge.

Say, "O my Lord! Advance me in knowledge."
(Ta Ha, 20: 114)

Say, 'Travel through the earth
And see how Allah originates creation,
then repeats it: truly that is easy for Allah.'
(The Spider, 29: 20)

Others take it literally, and go so far as to specify it as a wheat plant. They explain that, after Adam ate the fruit, he had a bowel movement and became conscious of his genitals; their shameful parts revealed to them, Adam and Eve stitched upon themselves leaves of the Garden (*Taha, 20: 121*). Personally I take the tree to be symbolic of sex and death that are ever associated in the story of biology. It was when living beings began to adopt copulation as a means of reproduction that death first came into the world; living beings did not copulate before that, but simply renewed themselves by division. Copulation was the forbidden tree that made life mortal. Adam's marriage to Eve had been originally one between immortals in Paradise, and they naturally had no use for copulation. Satan knew, however, that the tree of breeding meant the introduction of death and expulsion from the Garden of Immortals. He therefore lied to Adam. He tempted the couple to copulate by whispering to them that it was the tree of immortality.

As evidence of this view, let me refer the reader to the verse, cited above, where the Qur'an tells us that Adam and Eve felt ashamed and consequently covered their shameful parts with tree leaves. Surely no shame could be associated with the genitals until after the experience of sex. Children are never ashamed of their genitals, but adults hesitate even to mention them. The address to them after the act is in the plural, not the dual – two distinct cases in Arabic grammar:

> We said: "Get ye down, all (ye people),
> With enmity between yourselves.
> (The Heifer, 2: 36)

While the address before the sin was in the dual:

> And eat of the bountiful things therein
> As (where and when) ye will;
> But approach not this tree
> (The Heifer, 2: 35)

This means that eating the fruit of the tree led to reproduction. The pleasure of sex is to this day associated with profanity and animal desires. It is sex, rather than food, that is associated with temptation and the fall. It has been suggested that circumcision was the penance self-imposed by Adam, following the sin, an act of pseudo-castration, in disgust at what he had done; thus, its present status as a religious tradition.

On the other hand, the tree may indeed be an actual tree, the eating of which released the body's hormones, aroused sexual desires and led to Adam's and Eve's making love. This interpretation has the advantage of combining literal with figurative meanings. In matters like these, no absolute certainty may be attained because only God knows the truth, and the story of creation remains a great mystery. Still, I believe it is our duty to attempt to interpret such abstruse verses such as these because God commands us to try to understand.

> Say: "Travel through the earth
> And see how Allah did originate creation."
> (The Spider, 29: 20)

> Do they not look at the camels
> How they are made? –
> (The Overwhelming Event, 88: 17)

> Do they not then earnestly seek to understand
> The Qur'an, or are their hearts locked up by them?
> (Muhammad, 47: 24)

Indeed, it is our duty and responsibility to interpret the Qur'an and to make use of information made available to us by modern science. We must understand how it all began. Those who object to our evolutionary interpretation will inevitably ask: what can the fall mean – man's banishment from the Garden and the angels' bowing themselves down to Adam? Well, to fall (to go down, or get down) occurs in the Qur'an in the sense of moving from one place to another. It need not imply leaving the earth altogether. Thus God addresses the children of Israel:

Get ye down to any town and ye shall find what ye want
(The Heifer, 2: 61)

The Garden occurs elsewhere in the Qur'an to mean an orchard or an ordinary earthly garden:

There are for Saba,
Aforetime, a sign in their
Homeland – two Gardens
To the right and to the left
(Sheba, 34: 15)

And in the earth are tracts
(Diverse though) neighboring
And gardens of vines,
(The Thunder, 13: 4)

The fall must therefore be a moral fall – a falling from Grace – from a condition of bliss (where Adam had been honored by God) to a condition of misery (after Adam had disobeyed God and eaten from the forbidden tree.) The moral fall must have taken physical shape in Adam's expulsion from the easy life, perhaps to fertile lands and bounteous orchards, to the hard livelihood he now had to eke out in perhaps arid or barren land. He had been down here on earth all the while, of course, but never fell from any physical heaven.

The angels bowing themselves down to Adam must have taken place down here on earth as well. The act of bowing could be symbolic of the angels being placed in Adam's service by God's command, similarly as He put the *jinn* in Prophet Solomon's service. Or it could be that God wanted to reveal some of the

divine secrets to Adam, just as He revealed divine mysteries to
Muhammad on his night journey to Jerusalem and his ascension
to Heaven. These are miracles reserved by God for His prophets
and, as such, they reveal the high position in which God had
placed Adam. God had revealed all these things to Adam who
never left the earth.

It is the earth rather than Heaven that is our scene. God
created Adam, shaped him out of the finest branch of the tree of
life, planted him in the earth (grown out of the earth's clay), and
guided him up the scale of various breeds to the chosen apex – the
present shape of man. The following verses support this view:

> From the (earth) did We create you,
> And into it shall We return you.
> And from it shall We bring you
> Out once again.
> (Ta Ha, 20: 55)

> And Allah has produced you
> From the earth, growing (gradually),
> And in the End He will return you
> Into the (earth).
> (The Prophet Noah, 71: 17-18)

> He said: "Therein shall ye live,
> And therein shall ye die; but
> From it shall ye be taken out (at last)."
> (The Heights, 7: 25)

It is the earth from which we have never been away. The fall
may be a falling down from one place on the earth to another.

In another chapter of the Qur'an (Prostration) we can infer
the evolutionary idea from the way verses 32: 7, 8, and 9 are

made to suggest a sequence:

> *He who has made everything which He has created*
> *Most Good: He began the creation of man*
> *With (nothing more than) clay,*
> *And made his progeny from quintessence*
> *Of the nature of a fluid despised.*
> *But He fashioned him in due proportion, and breathed*
> *Into him something of His Spirit.*
> *And He gave you (the faculties of) hearing,*
> *And sight and feeling (and understanding):*
> *Little thanks do ye give!*
> *(The Prostration, 32: 7-9)*

In the beginning was the clay, then a progeny of mean water (or water despised, that is, semen), then the fashioning, the shaping up, and evolution across these progenies. Finally, there was the breathing in of the spirit – the mind, the inner self or conscience, freedom – into the acme of these progenies, man. Man must have developed further to acquire the faculties of hearing, sight, and feeling – the present highly developed man.

God mentions clay in the beginning, followed by the fashioning and the 'in-breathing'. Such a sequence must mean that Adam was not created at once out of clay but in stages; an interpretation based on the idea of evolution is therefore implied:

> *And Allah did create you from dust;*
> *Then from a sperm drop;*
> *then he made you in pairs.*
> *(The Originator of Creation, 35: 11)*

> *That He did create in pairs – male and female*
> *From a sperm drop when lodged (in its place)*
> *(The Star, 53: 45-46)*

The idea of falling down from heaven is refuted by the following verse:

It is He who hath produced you
From the earth and settled you therein
(The Prophet Hud, 11: 61)

Therein refers to the earth from which we are produced, which means that Adam came into being on earth and that the earth was subsequently given Adam to populate with his progeny. It is obvious that man's fall is purely moral – a fall from grace rather than a physical fall from Heaven:

It is He who sendeth down
Rain from the skies;
With it We produce
Vegetation of all kinds:
From some We produce
Green (crops), out of which
We produce grain
(The Cattle, 6: 99)

Could we infer from this verse that one breed came out of another rather than the independent creation of each?

Following the recent space probes, particularly man's landing on the moon, certain theories have been advanced about the origin of man. One says that man landed on the earth in a spacecraft in ancient times and that there is no link between man and the animal kingdom on earth for all their obvious similarities. According to that theory man came in the beginning from another planet.

This is, of course, pure hypothesis and surmise, a fiction akin to the fantasies of Jules Vernes and H.G. Welles. There is no basis of fact for it.

The controversy over the story of creation is interminable. The Qur'an neither supports nor denies the theory of evolution. The Qur'anic verses are capable of more than one interpretation and the subject is therefore a mystery that cannot be decided one way or the other. Indeed, science itself has not reached a final conclusion on this question.

It is in the context of the story of creation that God tells us about the seven heavens:

> *Allah is He who created seven Firmaments*
> *And of the earth a similar number*
> *(Divorce, 65: 12)*

> *He who created the seven heavens*
> *One above another*
> *(The Dominion, 67: 3)*

> *And We have made above you seven tracts*
> *(The Believers, 23: 17)*

> *And (have We not) built over you*
> *The seven firmaments?*
> *(The Great News, 78: 12)*

The question of the seven heavens is still a mystery which modern science has failed to unravel. But the figure *seven* itself makes one think: why should light consist of seven colors – the well-known spectrum bands modern science has established ? We know now that this scale of wavelengths, from red to violet, is repeated both in the infrared and ultra-violet areas. Similarly, the musical scale is composed of seven notes that are again repeated. Gynecologists tell us that a fetus becomes a fully-grown baby in the seventh month of pregnancy and that there is a risk of death if delivery occurs before that. From time immemorial, man has grouped the days into units of seven, and the week has been the established unit of measuring time. Without prior consultation or agreement, men of all colors and races and religions have accepted this. Why? How?

It has recently been discovered that the seven colors of sunlight (the spectrum) are caused by the transfer of electrons from one orbit to the next around the nucleus of the hydrogen atom. There are seven orbits. Every time the electron jumps from one orbit to the next, an electric charge is released; this accounts for a corresponding color of the spectrum.

These "jumps" occur in the body of the sun that consists of hydrogen. The tremendous heat (millions of degrees centigrade) forces the electrons to leave their atoms and radiate the white light of the sun. The electron therefore moves up the scale of seven orbits which are similar to the seven heavens. To move from one orbit to the next, the electron must break one of the energy bands attaching it to the nucleus. The energy thus released takes the form of a particular color of the spectrum. When the round of spectrum colors is completed, the electron finally leaves the atom.

This is as though the atom is a microcosm – a miniature model of the universe with its seven heavens! Does this mean that one day we shall discover that there is a seven-grade scale for every form of existence? Perhaps we shall discover a seven-grade pattern being repeated from top to bottom. The Qur'an often refers to the number '7' – Gehenna has seven doors. There are seven heavens and seven earths. We hear of Pharaoh's seven lean years and seven fat kind. We know that God completed creation on the seventh day. Couldn't all this point out one of the great mysteries of the universe?

There can be no doubt that the Qur'an is pointing in the direction of a highly important scientific question.

Let us take another example – a scientific point made by the Qur'an in the course of another verse:

> It is Allah who causeth the seed grain
> And the date stone to split and sprout.
> He causeth the living
> To issue from the dead
> And He is the One
> To cause the dead
> To issue from the living.
> (The Cattle, 6: 95)

Early commentators have explained that the verse refers to the splitting of the date stone at the point of growing into a new tree, which indeed means that a living trunk is coming out of a dead stone. Is it a coincidence that the cell also renews its life by the splitting of its nucleus, thus dividing into two cells? Note that the word nawat in Arabic means a nucleus as well as "stone" or "seed." Can it be a coincidence that an atom would not release its energy until its nucleus has been split (atomic fission) so that living energy is released from dead matter?

Another example:

> Glory to Allah, Who created
> In pairs all things that
> The earth produces, as well as
> Their own (human) kind
> And (other) things of which
> They have no knowledge.
> (Yaseen, 36: 36)

Man has always known that God created pairs, male and female, in the animal kingdom, but not that such a pattern exists as well in the inanimate world.

> *And of everything We have created pairs*
> *(The Winds That Scatter, 51: 49)*

In electricity we have both positive and negative charges. In magnetism we have two opposed poles. In the atom there are an electron and a proton and a neutron. In organic chemistry we have the sinistral and dextral parts.

Today we know all about matter and anti-matter. Science reveals to us daily more about such duality (the "pair structure") in all living organisms and inanimate objects. But in the Qur'an we already have a glimpse or glimpses of the existence of such a structure – a drop from the vast Qur'anic ocean, full as it is with mysteries.

One of the most profound of these mysteries concerns the Qur'anic description of the Day of Resurrection:

> *When the oceans boil over with a swell*
> *(The Folding Up, 81: 6)*

> *And when the earth is flattened out,*
> *And casts forth what is within it*
> *And becomes (clean) empty*
> *(The Rending Asunder, 84: 3-4)*

> *And by the Ocean filled with Swell –*
> *Verily, the Doom of the Lord*
> *Will indeed come to pass –*
> *(The Mount, 52: 6-7)*

Here is an oath by the ocean or the sea as it will be swarmed and set ablaze on the Day of Resurrection that God's chastisement will indeed take place. The oath draws attention to the importance of that event. The mystery of the sea aflame puzzled me for a long time. One day, while reading about volcanic activity, I came across a map prepared by a geologist showing the distribution of volcanic belts in the earth. This map started a series of reflections in a different direction.

The author, Dr. Poe, shows in chart after chart that most of the known 500 volcanoes are to be found in a circle round the Pacific Ocean, a line along the Mediterranean, and another line on the side of the Atlantic. More surprising, perhaps, is the discovery that the Pacific seabed consists of basalt that is a dark volcanic rock. This means that the burning inside of the earth is nearest to the surface at the seabed of the Mediterranean, the Pacific and Atlantic Oceans. These underwater areas are the weakest parts of the earth's crust, hence the eruption of volcanoes and the gushing out of lava from the inside to the surface. The author also lists the biggest volcanoes that make up the "ring of fire" around and under water. He specifies the volcanoes of Fujiyama, Mayon, Tal, Karkatoa, Orzaba, Parikutin, Kutu Paksi, Shimbo Razwa and the triad Mt. Lassen, Mt. Hood, and Mt. Rainer. There are also volcanic islands in the ocean such as the Hawaiian Islands where a tourist attraction is a place called Helioma or the House of Fire, which is literally a fire pit. Burning lava can be seen to pour forth incessantly, and fountains of molten rock gush out from the depths of the pit.

Of the Mediterranean volcanoes, the second largest (after Vesuvius) is Mt. Etna in Sicily. To the north of it, there is the Strampoli that is always active: every night it glows with reddish color, hence the name given to it by seamen – the Mediterranean Lighthouse. In the eastern Mediterranean, there is another group of volcanoes, including the Mt. Ararat. In the Atlantic, there are the Canaries, the Azores, and Cape Verde – all volcanic islands. A statistical fact provides conclusive evidence: 80% of all earthquake activity occurs in the same belt around the Pacific Ocean, and most earth tremors take place in the seabed.

The highest incidence of volcanic and earth tremor activity is to be found around and under water where the burning inside is nearest to the crust. It is prevented from causing a devastating explosion by the delicate balance in the earth's crust and the huge mountains which function as "weights" or "pegs" to keep the crust in position, to keep it firm; otherwise it would collapse into the surging sea of fire inside.

> He set on the earth mountains
> Standing firm, lest it shall shake with you
> And He scattered through it beasts of all kinds.
> We send down rain from the sky and produce
> On the earth every kind of noble creature, in pairs
> (Luqman, 31: 10)

Elsewhere the mountains are referred to as pegs (Al Naba, 78: 7). So, on the Day of Resurrection, when these mountains are blown up, the lava would gush out from the weak part in the crust, the seabed, and the earth would then be disemboweled of its burning inside.

> When the earth is shaken to its (utmost) convulsion
> And the earth throws up its burden (from within)
> (The Earthquake, 99: 1-2)

All the water of the sea and oceans will be aflame, hence that sea ablaze whose water had turned into fire:

> and Hell-Fire shall be placed
> in full view for all to see
> (Those Who Tear Out, 79: 36)

We know now that the temperature inside the earth is extremely high, that the center of the earth is a furnace of molten metal, rock, and lava. Perhaps, it is this inside that God means by His Hell:

> And to those straying in evil,
> The Fire will be placed in full view
> (The Poets, 26: 91)

To *be placed in full view* specifically means to take something from the inside to the surface, to make it visible. Perhaps this boiling inside is the lowest grade of inferno where the dense and dark souls will descend. Is this not the fire whose fuel is people and stones *(Prohibition 66: 6)*?

These hints and glimpses are profound words, where lofty eloquence combines with scientific accuracy. Such a combination cannot be a coincidence. It cannot be a coincidence that the eternal words of the Qur'an should be corroborated by the most recent scientific discoveries of our time.

Chapter 4

Heaven and Hell

One of the reasons why I turned my back on the Qur'an as a young man was the reference to the rivers of honey and wine in Paradise. As I liked neither, I concluded that these were naiveties. I eventually applied this conclusion to the Qur'an and to religion in general.

It was, in fact, I who was naive. I had not tried to understand the Qur'an. Not even the surface meaning of the words. I was hurried in my approach as though I really wanted to turn my back on it as soon as possible. It was, therefore, difficult for me to perceive the truth, plain though it was before me.

Now what does the Qur'an say about Paradise?

> *(Here is) a Parable of the Garden which*
> *The righteous are promised:*
> *In it are rivers*
> *Of water incorruptible,*
> *Rivers of milk*
> *Of which the taste never changes;*
> *Rivers of wine, a joy*
> *To those who drink;*
> *And rivers of honey*
> *Pure and clear.*
> *(Muhammad, 47: 15)*

The verse opens with a definite statement that it is a simile, a similitude, not a literal description of a place. This is only natural because both Heaven and Hell belong in the Unseen and can never be described literally. We simply have no linguistic machinery for this.

It is as though your child asked you about the pleasure of sex when he had no experience of it whatsoever. You would be hard-put to find the right words: how could you describe it indeed? Having exhausted all possible avenues, you might tell him, "Oh! It's as sweet as sugar!" Now this is a similitude taken from his immediate experience and daily life; yet how different are sex and sugar! That is precisely what the Qur'an did in addressing the simple Bedouin.

A Bedouin living in hot deserts would dream of nothing nicer than a spring of fresh water. Most of the springs he comes across are either salt or stale (stagnant). So is it with milk. How quickly does its taste change in the heat of the desert! And so the Qur'an strikes a similitude, using for vehicle the most sought-after object:

> *Allah disdains not to use*
> *The similitude of things,*
> *Lowest as well as highest.*
> *(The Heifer, 2: 26)*

The purpose is to approximate to the minds of the simple a complex (if not an impossible) concept of the Unseen. All references to Heaven and Hell must be seen in the context of analogy, a kind of approximation through similes and metaphors.

In the Bible, Joshua describes the Day of Grace in similar terms. St. Ephraim uses similar language in the incantations. Indeed, these are common images in all religions.

The Qur'an, however, does not leave us to struggle with nebulous similitudes. It soon sheds light on the subject.

> Now no person knows what delights of the eye
> Are kept hidden (in reserve) for them – as a reward
> For their (good) Deeds.
> (The Prostration, 32: 17)

The Qur'an shows us that the whole thing belongs in the Unseen that can never be expressed in earthly or human language. *Delights of the eye* is an imprecise expression. The original Arabic is a common metaphor equivalent to the English "warms the cockles of the heart" which is again an approximation of the meaning that is difficult to grasp in our language.

Hell is, on the other hand, horrific; it is neither death nor life.

> Death will come to him from every quarter,
> Yet will he not die: and in front of him will be
> A chastisement unrelenting.
> (The Prophet Abraham [Ibrahim], 14: 17)

> Fear the Fire, whose fuel is men and stones
> (The Heifer, 2: 24)

> They shall have Layers
> Of Fire above them,
> And Layers (of Fire)
> Below them: with this
> Doth Allah warn off
> His Servants: "O My Servants!
> Then fear ye Me!"
> (Crowds, 39: 16)

Now this is another fact presented by God: He is using these words to 'frighten' people. But it is not a baseless threat because this is precisely what happens when you warn your child not to neglect his teeth. "If you don't brush them, worms will eat them," you'd say, out of love, in the full knowledge that it won't be worms but rather invisible germs. Still, your threat was not baseless because the consequences of neglecting his teeth might prove worse than an onslaught by worms. Anyone who has experienced toothache will testify to that. Hence God warns of something that will definitely happen and will be more horrible than anything humanly imaginable.

Both retribution and reward are right. Some would object that it would be beneath God, in His unlimited capacity for forgiveness and mercy, to punish an insignificant person worth nothing in the scale of God's infinite Kingdom? This objection had bothered me for a long time and had made me reject the idea of punishment, and with it the Qur'an and religion as a whole.

What we need, in fact, is to ponder the concept of "punishment" more closely. God does not "punish" people. He causes them to suffer the consequences of what they have done, which is only fair. It is justice, rather than punishment, that we really have here. If in the other world, God equated the transgressor and the transgressed, the murderer with the victim on pretext of mercy, nothing would be farther from justice. To equate the unequal is to be grossly unjust, and God cannot be expected to be unfair.

Indeed, it would be anarchy itself if God were to regard all actions and people as equal. The order of the universe forbids it. Examine the universe and you will discover that perfect order and those infallible laws governing it. Every motion is calculated and everything is measured to a micron. The transfer of an electron from one orbit to the next within the atom is done with consummate precision. The electron must release a certain "energy band" equal to the leap it would make out of the orbit, then absorb another "energy band" equal to the leap back into position. Infinitesimal, invisible and almost insignificant, an electron is governed by a universal law and is accountable for its movements. Wouldn't that be expected of rational human beings who, compared with electrons, appear as vast as galaxies appear when compared to human beings? It is all the more befitting for man to be accountable for his action when God has breathed His Spirit into him and made him superior to all other beings when he is not as small as an atom or an electron!

Would it make sense if both wrongdoer and victim were reduced to dust after death forever, without hope of resurrection? Would all that a man's mind has earned and all that his soul has accomplished go in vain? It would simply be absurd!

> And they say: "What is
> There but our life
> In this world?
> We shall die and we live,
> And nothing but Time
> Can destroy us."
> But of that they have no
> Knowledge: they merely conjecture
> (The Kneeling Down, 45: 24)

Such conjecture is necessarily wrong, otherwise life would be an absurd play without meaning or purpose.

> Does man think
> That he will be left
> Uncontrolled (without purpose)?
> (The Resurrection, 75: 36)

A thinking mind could never accept such a conclusion: but would contemplate the creation of the universe and the perfect laws governing it:

> 'Our Lord! Not for naught
> Hast thou created [all] this!
> Glory to thee!'
> (The Family of 'Imran, 3: 191)

It is impossible that all this should come to nothing: there should be some kind of continuity, and we should find out the reason for all this in due course.

The question is, therefore, not one of retribution for the sake of retribution, but one of justice and logic.

> But ye have indeed rejected
> (Him) and soon will come
> The inevitable (punishment)!
> (The Criterion, 25: 77)

He who lives a wasteful life, refusing to hear, to see and reason out, and insisting on denying the truth when it is there in full view, will be resurrected deprived of sight:

> He will say, "O my Lord!
> Why hast thou raised me up blind,
> While I had sight (before)?"
> Allah will say: "Thus didst thou, when Our signs
> Came unto thee, disregard them:
> So wilt thou, this day, be disregarded."
> (Ta Ha, 20: 125-126)

It is simply something that you earn and which inevitably stays with you. God would not punish you; you would punish yourself by being ignorant:

> *We did them no wrong,*
> *But they were used to*
> *Doing wrong to themselves.*
> *(The Bees, 16: 118)*

He who lives as an animal in this world, with no interests apart from feeding and copulating, will have an animal existence in the other world, or, at least, an inferior position to those who have thought deeply:

> *But those who were blind in this world,*
> *Will be blind in the Hereafter,*
> *And most astray from the Path.*
> *(The Night Journey, 17: 72)*

In the other world differences will be greater, distinctions more prominent. Men will be distinguished by more than the usual differences between a human being and an animal.

> *See how We have bestowed*
> *More on some than on others;*
> *But verily the Hereafter*
> *Is more in rank and gradation*
> *And more in excellence.*
> *(The Night Journey, 17: 21)*

> *Soon will the wicked*
> *Be overtaken by*
> *Humiliation before Allah,*
> *And a severe punishment,*
> *For all their plots.*
> *(The Cattle, 6: 124)*

Such humiliation will be painful; it will burn and torture metaphorically, it will be a form of burning regret over what a man has missed and the comparison of his position with other people's gain will be a source of infinite torment for him.

> Our Lord! any whom Thou
> Dost admit to the Fire,
> Truly Thou coverest with shame
> (The Family of 'Imran, 3: 192)

Shame is regarded in this verse as more painful than fire. The Bible describes the other world as the world of "tears and teeth-grinding" (Matthew 8: 12) – when a sinner will grind his teeth in regret over his humiliation especially as compared with the superior position of others. The Qur'an describes the good souls in Paradise as those nearest to God, nearest to the Truth:

> In an Assembly to Truth
> In the Presence of
> A Sovereign Omnipotent.
> (The Moon, 54: 55)

We are told that God speaks to them and looks at them. We are also told that they are established on symbolic "thrones," facing each other, that is, having shed the low, little worldly hatreds, they are now loving brothers. Heaven is described as the "home of peace," free from war, lies, bad language, and idle talk. The Qur'an describes the gardens of Eden, pointing out the goodly dwelling places and rivers, etc., then concludes by saying that the believers will enjoy, better than all this, God's satisfaction:

> But the greatest bliss
> Is the good pleasure of Allah:
> That is supreme felicity.
> (The Repentance, 9: 72)

The position of the believers is gauged not by their physical pleasures, but more importantly in effect, by being capable of enjoying God's good pleasure. The same idea is stressed in the following verse that recommends prayer at night:

> And pray in the small watches
> Of the morning: (it would be)
> An additional prayer
> (Or spiritual profit)
> For thee: soon will thy Lord
> Raise thee to the Station
> Of Praise and Glory.
> (The Night Journey, 17: 79)

It is essentially a question of level or rank, and each man is assigned a definite one in the other world.

To recapitulate, punishment is used not for the sake of punishment. The sense of torment, of excruciating pain, comes from the feeling that one has sunk so low, that one is inevitably humiliated and must live with one's eternal loss, in envy of the others who have been spared that loss. Such a feeling should burn up sinners' hearts more than any physical fire would; it is a kind of self-punishment one has in consequence of the position he has earned by wrong-doing in this world.

That Hell-fire is different from the fire of this world is shown by the following verses:

> And they will bear witness against themselves
> That they were unbelievers. He will say,
> 'Enter among nations that passed
> Away before you, jinn and mankind,
> Into the Fire.' Whenever any nation
> Enters, it curses its sister-nation; till, when

They have all successively come there,
The last of them shall say to the first of
Them, 'O our Lord, these led us astray:
So give them a double chastisement of
The fire.' He will say, 'Unto each a
Double but you know not.'
(The Heights, 7: 37-38)

It is a dialogue in Hell between the unbelievers while being tortured by the burning fire. Can such a dialogue take place in our kind of worldly fire? Certainly not. Furthermore, "unto each a double" means that each individual of the earlier nation is taking double the punishment of the later nation while roasting in the same fire. And, *"but you know not,"* means clearly that the source of pain is not the place of the psyche. Not that the torment is not physical; but it is probably moral as well. Two people may be subjected to the same scorching heat in this world; one may get a headache, while the other may escape unscathed. A headache may be both physical and psychological. Again, the reference may be indeed to a real fire, but it must be different from our own.

The Qur'an describes the Gardens of Paradise in detail. We learn that the believers will be given fruits to eat like those they had known on earth (though with a difference in quality, of course.) They will have companions whose love has been perfected.

But give glad tidings
To those who believe
And work righteousness,
That their portion is Gardens,
Beneath which rivers flow.
Every time they are fed

With fruits therefrom,
They say: "Why, this is
What we were fed with before,"
For they are given things in similitude;
And they have therein
Companions pure (and holy);
And they abide therein (forever).
(The Heifer, 2: 25)

As such, Heaven must be only a station or position. It contains all we know on earth but vastly differs in degree. The difference is, however, unimaginable, like the difference between temporality and eternity, the difference (mentioned earlier) between the taste of sugar and sexual pleasure. The same thing applies to the Qur'anic references to fire, which must be different from the fire we know. In Hell, a tree, the *Zaqoum*, grows and bears thorny fruit. There is also boiling water to be drunk, and the people there talk and converse with each other. Their bodies should not have the same chemistry as ours, otherwise they would evaporate in seconds.

This means that we are going to be resurrected in bodily form but with vastly different bodies. We may be shaped in the same way but molded from a different material that must remain unknown to us. At any rate, we will not have the same earthly bodies as we have in this world. Pleasures may multiply, physically, and morally, in a mysterious way; and so may pain. And as people will be divided according to rank and category, each will have a corresponding degree of happiness or misery. I believe the highest ranks will be reserved for those who snub sensual pleasures and the sensuous Paradise; the All-Merciful will give them the privilege of pure spiritual life near to Him at the *Lote*

Tree. No pleasure could be drawn there from food or drink but only from contemplating the perfection of God, from reflecting on the Truth, the beauty, of the ultimate and absolute good.

> *In an Assembly to Truth*
> *In the Presence of*
> *A Sovereign Omnipotent*
> *(The Moon, 54: 55)*

It is the position of the favored, the Prophets and those of similar rank.

There are all sorts of ranks in Heaven, beginning from the low sensuous pleasures of food and drink, rising to the high spiritual pleasures that are pure and super sensuous.

To recapitulate, Hellfire is not our kind of fire. Paradise is not exactly a fruit seller's shop. Nor is God in any sense a tyrant. Indeed, God is the fairest judge of all because He maintains for humankind the stations or ranks consciously and deliberately earned by them in this world. Pain will result from the recognition of such ranks and from being subjected to a lower position than that of others forever and ever. The final position of each will be as fixed as his fingerprint. And the pain will be real, almost visible.

> *Nay, were ye to know*
> *With certainty of mind,*
> *(Ye would beware!)*
> *Ye shall certainly see Hellfire!*
> *Again ye shall see it*
> *With certainty of sight!*
> *(The Piling Up, 102: 5-7)*

Because God knows that this pain will be great, He has warned and frightened us. He uses most expressive words, and He sends down messengers to warn and bring good tidings supported by miraculous deeds, Signs, and Scriptures. He does so because He is All-Merciful. He is extending a hand of mercy, kindness, and love. In a *Qudsi* verse (an address by God to Muhammad outside the Qur'an), God says, "My mercy comes before my wrath." In the *Fatiha*, the opening chapter of the Qur'an, He says that He is All-Merciful, All-Compassionate and then proceeds to say that He is the Master of the Day of Doom, the Day of Judgment, the Day of Wrath, when all people will be called to account, once and for all. Because He is merciful, God keeps the door wide open for repentance, for redressing any wrongs committed.

> *Say: O my servants who*
> *Have transgressed against their souls!*
> *Despair not of the Mercy*
> *Of Allah: for Allah forgives*
> *All sins for He is*
> *Oft-Forgiving, Most Merciful.*
> *(Crowds, 39: 53)*

> *But without doubt, I am*
> *(Also) He that forgives*
> *Again and again, to those*
> *Who repent, believe,*
> *And do right – who,*
> *In fine, are ready to receive*
> *True guidance.*
> *(Ta Ha, 20: 82)*

After commanding the believers to observe their prayers, God goes on to say that the remembrance of God is, without doubt, the greatest thing in life (*The Spider, 29:45*). In other words, you must always remember that there is Divine Power, that this idea be always present in your mind and reflected in your deeds. This will help you and secure your devotion as a believer; it will be better than a prayer devoid of God's remembrance.

The Arabic word for remember, to be reminded or admonished, is *dhikr*. It is a difficult word to translate, though we continually obscure its meaning. The Qur'an itself is called *Dhikr*, to believe or be capable of admonishment is to remember. The following verses are given in two translations; the first preserves the original literal *dhikr*, and the second gives a variant in the light of its particular context:

> 1. *Only men possessed of minds remember.*
> *(Crowds, 39: 9)*
>
> It is only those endowed with understanding
> That receive admonition.
>
> 2. *And when reminded, they do not remember.*
> *(The Ranged in Ranks, 37: 13)*
>
> And when admonished, they pay no heed.
>
> 3. *It is We who have sent down the*
> *remembrance, and We watch over it.*
> *(Al Hijr, 15: 9)*
>
> We have, without doubt,
> Sent down the Message. And We will assuredly
> Guard it from corruption.
>
> 4. *Now We have made the Qur'an easy for Remembrance.*
> *Is there any that will remember?*
> *(The Moon, 54: 17)*

And We have indeed
Made the Qur'an easy
To understand and remember
Then is there any that will receive admonition?

5. Then remind them! Thou art only a reminder;
thou are not charged to oversee them.
(The Overwhelming Event, 88: 21)

Therefore do thou give admonition,
For Thou art one to admonish.

6. A Book We have sent down to thee,
Blessed, that men possessed of
minds may ponder its signs and so remember.
(Saad, 38: 29)

(Here is) a Book which
We have sent down
Unto thee, full of blessings
That they may meditate on its signs,
And that Men of understanding may
Receive admonition.

7. The God fearing, when a visitation of
Satan troubles them, remember,
And then they see clearly.
(The Heights, 7: 20)

Those who fear God.
When a thought of evil
From Satan assaults them
Bring God to remembrance
when lo! they see aright!

With minor alterations, the first of each pair of the variants is Professor Arberry's and the second is Yusuf Ali's. The first keeps the original meaning of the Arabic word regardless of context; the second adjusts that meaning to suit the position of the word in each sentence. But even so, most contexts call for the original sense to be preserved, namely that of memory, remembrance, reminding.

A long pause is required to ponder this 'sense': what kind of remembrance is it that is needed or ordered?

The most recent psychological theory tells us that all knowledge is hidden within the psyche, but heavily veiled by instincts and desires. Learning is in effect a remembrance, a lifting of the veils thrown by worldly existence on the psyche. There is no such thing as acquiring knowledge from a void mind. When a child is told that 2+2=4, he does not acquire any external information: he simply remembers an inborn piece of information. Similarly, the appreciation of beauty and music is a kind of vague remembrance of the Divine Kingdom, man's prenatal existence in the spiritual world.

A woman's beauty is, therefore, only transient, never abiding. Indeed, it is not her own beauty, but a reflection from the Divine Kingdom. When the law of thick matter, of old age and earthly dust takes its course, her beauty goes.

Before we were born we had lived as spirits. As the previously quoted beautiful verse says, the Lord made them testify concerning themselves:

> "Am I not your Lord?
> (Who cherishes and sustains you?)"–
> They said: "Yea! We do testify."
> (The Heights, 7: 172)

The verse relates what happens in the Unseen world before earthly creation. All creatures that God made, makes, and will make are made to testify that He is their Lord. They all admit it, and God takes compact with them because He knows that after they are born they will forget, perhaps totally forget, where they came from. The physical veil of the body is thick enough to blind them to the truth, so that they cannot remember. In His mercy, God sends down prophets to remind them. He tells Muhammad:

> *Therefore do thou give admonition,*
> *For thou art one to admonish.*
> *(The Overwhelming Event, 88: 21)*

God refers to belief or faith as a kind of life because it links earthly existence, through remembrance, with existence at the higher spiritual plane before birth. It also links this world with immortality in the other world, and make the person conscious of one's life in its totality. It is life itself.

> *O ye who believe!*
> *Give your response to Allah*
> *And His Messenger, when he*
> *Calleth you to that which*
> *Will give you life*
> *(The Spoils of War, 8: 24)*

God is in no need of our prayers or our fasting. It is we who need them to remind us of the source of our existence, and to help us to draw on the ultimate source of life. Worship is an attempt to draw on divine power, which we need to live. We cannot live unless we actually draw on this power, the power of the living God.

It follows that God has ordained worship for our own good, not to make Him feel His Divine Power; indeed, He has no need of us, no need to punish us, no need to make requests or ordain anything.

> *What can Allah gain*
> *By your punishment,*
> *If ye are grateful*
> *And ye believe?*
> *(The Women, 4: 147)*

In other words, there is no pleasure or advantage to God in punishing His own creatures, over whom He watches with loving care. He indeed does not ordain or request anything, or even punish us; this is suggested merely by the surface meaning of the words, but the inner meaning that reveals itself only to those who work hard enough is different. God is merciful and His mercy absolute. He is just and His justice absolute. He is the giver and His generosity absolute. He does not take anything because He does not need anything.

The variety of punishment in this world should be regarded as an expression of God's kindness and mercy:

> *And indeed We will make*
> *Them taste of the Penalty*
> *Of this (life) prior to*
> *The supreme Penalty in order*
> *That they may (repent and) return.*
> *(The Prostration, 32: 21)*

God attempts to awaken the minds of those who still have time to remember and see the light. To suffer lesser woes can, therefore, save a man's soul from the greater woes of the other world.

The Qur'an tells us that God means to awaken the heedless by making them suffer all kinds of worldly plights – poverty, disease, and pain – so that they may realize the transience of this world and the immortality of the other. He does it because He is merciful, and because He knows that the law by which they are to be judged is merciless in the end. If they suffer all these, however, without waking up to the reality, God may give them a different kind of trial: money! They would enjoy this life to the full, and then have to face the horrors of real pain, everlastingly, in the other world:

> *Before thee We sent*
> *(Messengers) to many nations,*
> *And We afflicted the nations*
> *With suffering and adversity*
> *That they might learn humility.*
> *When the suffering reached*
> *Them from Us, why then*
> *Did they not learn humility?*
> *On the contrary their hearts*
> *Became hardened, and Satan*
> *Made their (sinful) acts*
> *Seem alluring to them.*
> *But when they forgot*
> *The warning they had received*
> *We opened to them the gates*
> *Of all (good) things,*
> *Until, in the midst*
> *Of their enjoyment*
> *Of Our gifts*
> *On a sudden, We called*
> *Them to account, when lo!*
> *They were plunged in despair!*
> *(The Cattle, 6: 42-44)*

What appears to be a blessing may in fact be a plight.

Let not their wealth
Nor their (following in) sons
Dazzle thee; in reality
Allah's Plan is to punish them
With these things in this life,
And that their souls may perish
In their (very) denial of Allah.
(The Repentance, 9: 55)

Do they think that because
We have granted them abundance
Of wealth and sons
We would hasten them
On in every good? Nay
They do not understand.
(The Believers, 23: 55-56)

Worldly wealth, power and influence may be but trials. Let not their possessors think that they are in themselves things that will bring them happiness.

We grant them respite
That they may grow
In their iniquity
(The Family of 'Imran, 3: 178)

Apparent "good" things in this world should not always be taken as a sign of God's satisfaction, nor should suffering imply God's wrath. "Abundance" may indicate divine wrath, and a plight may be an expression of mercy. The truth cannot be ascertained except by reference to the inner voice, your conscience. If you believe that a plight has "purified" your soul, it must be a blessing in disguise; if worldly gifts turn you into a rebel against God, they must indicate His wrath.

The Qur'an describes the people of Hell:

Those against whom the Word
Of thy Lord hath been verified
Would not believe –
Even if every Sign was brought
Unto them – until they see
(For themselves) the Grievous Penalty.
(The Prophet Jonah [Yunus], 10: 96-97)

Having seen the painful chastisement, they will say:

"Would that we were
But sent back!
Then would we not reject
The Signs of our Lord,
But would be amongst those
Who believe."

But if they were returned
They would certainly relapse
To the things they were forbidden
For they are indeed liars.
(The Cattle, 6: 27-28)

God knows that if returned to this world (if allowed, that is, to reassume the fleshy robes they had discarded) they would resume their earlier position of proud rejection. They are not merely ignorant because the ignorant can learn. Indeed, they are arrogant because they refuse to recognize the Truth. They are incorrigible because nothing could make them relent, not even God's prophets, His miracles, and not even His fire. They should be made to suffer the penalty of fire physically. This, being capable of making them feel the Truth, must be seen as a sign of God's mercy.

God is always merciful, even when He punishes with fire. He is the All-Merciful, that is, He is merciful at all times and to all people, both worthy and unworthy. The worthy will go to Heaven and the unworthy to Hell because fire is a means of imparting knowledge to the hard-hearted and thick-headed people who could never otherwise be made to learn the Truth. Indeed, fire is an expression of mercy. One of the most beautiful verses reads:

> He said: "With my Punishment
> I visit whom I will;
> But My mercy extendeth
> To all things.
> (The Heights, 7: 156)

His chastisement is indicated as a form of mercy; His mercy embraces everything. Of the reckoning God says:

> "Read thine (own) record;
> Sufficient is thy soul
> This day to make out
> An account against thee."
> (The Night Journey, 17: 14)

Reckoning appears to be a form of self-reckoning, self-confrontation, and self-punishment. The work of each individual will be hung on him like his shadow, and there will be no escape when sentence is passed and eternal justice done.

These ideas are concealed from us because we read the Qur'an in haste or because we enjoy the sound of the words, heedless of their meaning. But the sound of the words, often awesome and impressive, is functional. The words employed to describe the Day of Resurrection are particularly awe-inspiring and echoes loudly right through one's ears. That Day is referred to as The

Hour, The Terror, The Clatterer, The Earth-Tremor, The Crusher, The Enveloper, The Shiverer, The Scare, The Agony, The Catastrophe, The Indubitable, and The Blast. The Arabic word for *Blast* is unbelievably awesome; it could pierce your eardrum! God knows that man is usually lured away from the Truth by the business of this world, his desires and ambitions, and is often unmindful and deaf to reasoning. He needs to listen to such words; perhaps they would awaken his lethargic mind:

> *At length, when there*
> *Comes the Deafening Noise –*
> *That Day shall a man*
> *Flee from his own brother,*
> *And from his mother,*
> *And his father,*
> *And from his wife,*
> *And his children.*
> *(He Frowned, 80: 33-36)*

To recapitulate, God's punishment is an expression of His loving care and great mercy. It is never imposed for the sake of punishment. Punishment is the fulfillment of certain conditions, justly and inevitably. It means that men's souls would be graded in accordance with the ranks they had already earned by their own work on this earth. It should mark the final curtain to this world where people are vying to make undeserved gains.

Let us illustrate such difference in rank by examples from everyday life. We feel, don't we, that we are not equal in rank? Here the word "rank" refers to the quality of human existence rather than to income or the standard of living. One may live at a physical level only, trying to satisfy his body's requirements, aiming at nothing higher than eating, drinking, and copulating.

One may quench that physical thirst but fall prey to another, a psychological thirst involving jealousy, envy, anger, schaden-freude, eminence, fame, power, the hoarding of money, fighting for domination, and higher posts. Most people do not rise above this rank and their minds are used only to help them achieve these ends.

For most people, life is a jungle. Their natural emotion is aggression, and they are constantly fighting for survival, struggling to get anything on which they can lay their hands. They swing, pendulum-like, from one desire to another, inflamed by allurements and endless ambitions.

A few people can, however, discover the falsehood of this life and wake up to the realization that this kind of existence involves more slavishness than freedom. Such a life would look like hard labor or slave labor being dictated by savage, insatiable instincts and inane, insignificant, and worthless mortal ambitions. They set about silencing the ugly cries of the body and curbing their wild internal desires, as both the cries and the desires distort their vision and understanding. They do this by substituting love for hate and giving for taking. They gradually rise in rank in the sense indicated in earlier passages. Eventually they reach a state of serenity and inner peace. They may now look back in anger, disgusted at having been their own slaves, driven around senselessly in a mad infernal vicious circle. In the end, they are truly liberated; they have saved their spirits and recognized the truth, namely, that they had been undergoing a test, a trying experience.

In rank the body may be comparable to dust, the soul to fire, the spirit to light. This is just an approximation; but, even as a metaphor, it does show that the business of ranks is very real. A rank a man has earned in this world is kept by him in the other, which is only fair. It is not tyranny.

The pain would be indescribable if the souls had shed their earthly bodies, leaving nothing behind but pure, anomalistic and rabid hunger, burning, insatiable, and naked desires; and animosity growing among fierce souls, destined to be at war forever, without hope of truce or peace. On the other hand, there will be the spirits of the few who will live in love and contemplate the truth in the divine Kingdom.

I should definitely state that the awful-sounding descriptions of Hell constitute a warning of a real, indescribable self-inflicted pain; and the pain will be inflicted in accordance with the work done in this world. I almost see this as the absolute and certain truth. "Far be it from God," as Milton would say, to punish for the sake of punishment. God is the Truth and the Fairest Judge.

Chapter 5

Lawful and Unlawful

The Qur'an makes nothing lawful or unlawful without reason. It makes lawful all that is good for man, and unlawful all that is bad:

For He commands them
What is just and forbids them
What is evil; He allows
Them as lawful what is good
(And pure) and prohibits them
From what is bad (and impure)
(The Heights, 7: 157)

God forbids all that is harmful, but allows all that is useful. The Qur'anic law is not a wanton law designed to make life difficult for people. On the contrary, it is an expression of infinite love and mercy. Failure to grasp this basic fact will land us in a labyrinth of interminable details, and the true spirit of the Qur'an will be lost to us.

Say to the believing men
That they should lower their gaze
And guard their modesty
And say to the believing women
That they should lower
Their gaze and guard their modesty
(The Light, 24: 30-31)

The verse appears to make life difficult for us. Why should God grant us eyes but command us not to see? Why did He create beauty if we are commanded not to enjoy it? If we look for a deeper than literal meaning, we shall find that such a command actually saves a man from a wicked kind of slavery and is, as such, an expression of God's kindness to us. Apart from being improper (or against good manners), staring is the prelude to attachment, and to be attached is to be the prisoner of a passion. The only way to freedom, we now know, is to go beyond sensuous pleasures in search of the sublime principles in God's creation. Seeking the Creator in His creation will bring us nearer to God and make us hopeful of attaining absolute freedom.

Worldly temptations are made to test us and establish whether we would act according to the healthy principles of our human nature or attach ourselves to the inferior, sensuous beauty of earthlings? If we do the latter, we would prove that something was wrong with our inclinations, wrong enough to divert us from freedom to slavery. The question is neither simply one of a beautiful face nor one of a casual look. The stare may engender a feeling, followed by a desire and, perhaps, a plan of satisfying the desire by possessing the object of the desire. The mind may fall prey to the desire and the man may literally lose his way. He may simply seek the woman in question, forgetful of what he had originally set out to do. Such a man will have lost his freedom and fallen from his humanity to the animal position of a dog on the scent. Unable to free himself from the bonds of that bosom or those legs, his mind would be lost in the anticipated pleasures of sex. With a watering mouth and bulging eyes, he would forget all about his work, lose control, and allow a pair of trembling feet to take him where the flesh ordains. If actually taking place in the street, this incident may come to an end with his face being slapped or with an actual love affair beginning with pleasure but ending with slavery, if not with a robbery or a sexually transmitted disease requiring medical treatment.

The ruling by the Qur'anic verse on this kind of stare is obvious. In fact, good taste naturally forbids it because of its harmful possibilities. The Qur'an commands believing women to draw their veils over their bosoms (*The Light, 24: 31*) in order to avoid possible temptation to men.

This is the essential principle of forbidding. The reason for prohibition is always the harm something does. God has established His law on the basis of love and mercy, not on tyranny and despotism. Consequently, to cast down one's eyes is to avoid possible harm and to protect oneself from the weakness innate in our physical nature.

As a principle, casting down one's eyes does not apply only to women's bodies but also to other people's possessions. It implies that a believer should not covet other people's property but put himself above low desires of envy, jealousy, and hate.

One of the most heinous sins in the eyes of God is fanaticism. To be a fanatic means that a person is narrow-minded. A person is often prejudiced in favor of his own family if not indeed for himself alone, and prejudice often entails vanity and pride. Above all, a fanatic is a person who worships himself and his limited understanding of life, rather than God. He is, therefore, really an unbeliever. The quintessence of religion is to go beyond yourself, to renounce it. The surest way of achieving this is, of course, to control your desires, harness your prejudices, free yourself from your ambitions, and throw aside your vanity, pride, and self-involvement. These are shackles that our religion regards as unlawful because Islam seeks to liberate the human soul from bondage.

The worst and most odious form of lawlessness, in the eyes of God, is polytheism, that is, the worship of things other than God. Polytheism is not the worship of pagan idols pure and simple; this is an old, naive kind of paganism that is dead and buried. Today's idols are not the pre-Islamic idols of ancient Arabia– al-Laat, al-'Uzzah and Hubal! Today, we have abstract idols worshiped everywhere, the worst to be found. The most dangerous form of idolatry is to make an idol of yourself and worship your own opinions, prejudices and interests.

> Then seest thou such a one as takes
> As his God his own vain desire?
> (The Kneeling Down, 45: 23)

Self is the god of today's world, to whom incense is being burned and sacrificial blood (of others) is being offered. Applying the criterion of unlawfulness, we may ask, What harm can this do? Is there any harm in self-worship? There is in fact, nothing but harm! A self-worshipper cannot lead a normal life. He spends his days in a prison of mirrors so that wherever he looks he must see his image reflected. He would lie, steal, kill, and exploit others. He cannot listen to the cries of others because of the walls that he has erected around himself, nor can he see anyone but himself – his gains, his property, and his material wealth. And it is nothing apart from his very self that would constitute the walls around him. Shut in within these walls, he can have no vision of the truth, justice or God.

Of such people, the Qur'an has the following to say:

> And We have put a bar in front of them
> And a bar behind them,

And further We have covered them up;
So they cannot see.
(Yaseen, 36: 9)

The barrier is nothing but yourself. The Qur'an says in a different context:

But he hath made no haste
On the path that is steep;
And what will explain
To thee the path that is steep? –
(It is:) freeing the bondman;
(The City, 90: 11-13)

The reader is asked about the steep path. He is required to think about it himself. This is a difficult question, but elsewhere we are helped to understand that the steep path is the path of the self. There is no hurdle before you depart from that one. The only way to get over it is to do good work. The work suggested is the freeing of someone in bondage. But couldn't that be symbolic? For you to free your bondsman is to be aware of the idea of bondage. You may realize that you are in bondage yourself and therefore try to break your own bonds. Can you succeed in freeing a human being without having freed yourself first? Once successful, however, you'll realize that you are, after all, capable of good work. You could love and contribute to life around you and your fellow beings. This is the intent of the following verses:

Allah hath purchased of the Believers
Their persons and their goods;
For theirs (in return)
Is the Garden (of Paradise)
(The Repentance, 9: 111)

So turn (in repentance) to your Maker,
And slay yourselves (the wrongdoers);
That will be better for you
In the sight of your Maker.
(The Heifer, 2: 54)

The original word for *mortify* in Arabic may be rendered as "kill" or "slay" (as many translators of the Qur'an have done) but the meaning is obvious. The divine command is for the sinners to humiliate their souls (not to kill themselves), and for all human beings to defeat the low desires of the self and emerge victorious against themselves. In the Bible, Jesus Christ says something to this effect. God advises David to make an enemy of himself. When David asked how to reach God, the answer was, "Leave yourself and come to me." In the Qur'an, God says to Moses:

"Verily I am thy Lord!
Therefore (in My presence)
Put off thy shoes: thou art
In the sacred valley Tuwa."
(Ta Ha, 20: 12)

You cannot be truly in the presence of God until you have cast off your self, that is, both your physical appendage (and needs) and your world preoccupations (the shoes stand for both.)

That is why self-worship is a kind of secret idolatry. It is the topmost forbidden thing and highest sin because it entails all other sin and leads to consummate destruction. You would be a disbeliever if you worship anything other than God. If you are the slave of your self, your desires and interests; your family or tribal prejudice, racist or ethnic pride; an abstract idea or a theory to the extent that you refuse to consider any other, you would be, especially in the last case, worshipping an idol, albeit an abstract one, carved out of philosophy rather than of matter. Understandably, the Qur'an regards polytheism as an unforgivable sin. It blinds both the eye and mind, paralyses the senses, and stunts the growth of the spirit because it obstructs the spiritual journey to the source of light.

> *Allah forgiveth not*
> *That partners should be set up*
> *With Him; but He forgiveth*
> *Anything else, to whom He pleaseth.*
> *(The Women, 4: 48)*

Polytheism means in effect the disruption of the umbilical cord that maintains the vital link between the embryo and its source of life, between man and God. Can you imagine what might happen if a sunflower turned its back on the sun, preferring to face the moon, for instance? Would it not die? It does not worship the sun because of the flower's lowly station in life, but because the sun gives it life.

> *O ye who believe!*
> *Give your response to Allah*
> *And His Messenger, when He*
> *Calleth you to do that which*
> *Will give you life.*
> *(The Spoils of War, 8: 24)*

Worship is life and a seeking of light and truth. God has ordained worship because he knows it to be the source of our life; he did not order it for the sake of giving orders.

It is not surprising, therefore, that God has forbidden us to drink alcohol or take intoxicating drugs because their harmful effect is obvious. Gambling is likewise forbidden on account of the financial loss it incurs and the hate it engenders. Fornication is forbidden because it involves promiscuity and anarchy. It disturbs family life by allowing transient and vain desires to rule supreme. On the other hand, marriage is made lawful because it entails an order, where it allows man to bear his responsibilities, have a sense of discipline, and enjoy peace of mind. Pork is forbidden because the pig is a carrier of the influenza virus and the tapeworm, and its flesh consists of the toughest and most complex protein (amino acids). While all herbivores, such as gazelles, rabbits, horses, camels, poultry, and even donkeys are gentle and meek, carnivores are, on the contrary, fierce, ferocious, and ruthless. These might include lions, tigers, hyenas, wolves, foxes, vultures, and hawks, to name a few. There can be no doubt that a greater proportion of meat in the diet is associated with certain psychological qualities such as ferocity, ruthlessness, and sharp temper. Because pork is the toughest and most complex animal protein, its harm may be greater than all other kinds of meat. Only God knows; we don't.

God is the All-Encompassing, Comprehensive Mind. He ordains nothing without a reason. He has established His law, specified what is lawful and what isn't, and ordained worship, out of loving care and mercy. We must always be conscious of this fact because it is the spirit of divine law.

Robbery is forbidden, and so is murder.

If anyone slew a person – unless it be
For murder or for spreading mischief in the land –
It would be as if he slew the whole people:
And if anyone saved a life, it would be as if he saved
The life of the whole people.
(The Repast, 5: 32)

Wanton murder is tantamount to breaking all the laws, and God regards it as equal to the killing of all people. God also forbids self-slaughter (suicide):

Nor kill (or destroy)
Yourselves: for verily
Allah hath been to you
Most Merciful!
If any do that
In rancor and injustice –
Soon shall We cast them
Into the Fire: and easy
It is for Allah.
(The Women, 4: 29-30)

To commit suicide in a premeditated way is to have the most evil thought of God, to be blinded to His mercy, to despair of His justice, to break His laws, and to deny His other world. It is the greatest iniquity one can inflict on himself.

And that He may punish
The Hypocrites, men and
Women, and the Polytheists,
Men and women, who imagine
An evil opinion of Allah
On them is a round
Of Evil: the wrath of Allah
Is on them; He has cursed
Them and got Hell ready
For them: and evil
Is it for a destination.
(The Victory, 48: 6)

As has been mentioned, God forbids fornication because of its harm. A modern Western liberal may question what harm it can do? What possible harm could there be if two adults agreed to enjoy the pleasures of sex outside wedlock but behind closed doors? They would, wouldn't they, be honest with themselves if they kept clear of everybody's way and did it as an act of love? What possible harm could this do?

To realize the "harm" involved, we must establish the natural framework of love and sex. Nature has intended that particular emotion, with the ensuing love act, as a means of reproduction for the survival for the human species and the peopling of the world. Love is therefore a means of reproduction. When a man and a woman, on the other hand, seek a sequestered corner to have sex without planning to have a home and a family of their own (but merely, that is, to steal a secret pleasure), they will be distorting the natural character of love and sex. To use modern terminology, instead of being functional as a means of reproduction, sex will be practiced much like a consumer good. The couple would thus be consuming, or wasting, a God-given, honorable, vital energy. Though intended for the spread of civilization by the progeny of humankind, this energy will be reduced to a means of inducing stupid and insipid sexual quivers!

When two men agree to indulge in homosexuality, they will advance the same argument in defense. They will tell you, "We are here of our own free will. We love one another. We hurt no one. We are having pleasure but harm nobody at all!" Readers will admit more readily, I am sure, that this gay case is abnormal but there is abnormality in both cases. We should always be mindful of the universal law that governs all things. Both cases represent a deviation of the natural energy from its prescribed outlets in return for a few minutes of sexual quivers. The difference being only in degree, the degree of their repulsiveness and violation of the law of nature. The former couple who claim to be honest with themselves are utterly dishonest and untruthful, because you cannot be honest and true to yourself unless you are true to human nature and to nature in the widest sense of the term. If a man acts against his nature, he may be split in two parts and sadly break up into a body divorced from his soul.

If truly in love with a man, a woman should not say, "I'd like to go to bed with you," but rather, "I'd like to live with you all my life. I want you to be the father of my children. I want you to share my home and be an honor to my name as a constant companion throughout the journey of my life." If not, she would be lying too.

She would be wrong, even if she claimed to be a Juliet. The sinner who prostitutes herself for a livelihood may have something to say for herself (she may claim to be utterly destitute), but the sinner who pollutes the most honorable natural gift in this way will have nothing to say in defense, having had no motive beyond transient quivers and silly convulsions! It is an itch that requires periodic sedatives in the name of love. A woman in love will seek a father for her children and a roof over her head, not a temporary treatment for the itch.

If turned into a habit, a regular conduct, and a way of life, fornication must result in the utter disintegration of a person's character to a kind of split personality bordering on schizophrenia. The body would go in one direction, the heart in another, and the spirit nowhere! Man's nature (human nature itself) would be destroyed. Here lies the danger. This is what explains the highest incidence of lunacy and suicide in Sweden and Russia, notwithstanding the sexual satisfaction and utter permissiveness of the young. Where inner peace is lost, in consequence of permissiveness, man's nature becomes unbalanced and madness sets in.

Religious teachings have, therefore, more profound reasons than appear at a cursory glance. They have practical purposes and material uses.

Why is marriage forbidden between a brother and sister, a mother and child, a father and daughter? Our religion inspires love other than passion to grow in the family: maternal, paternal, and fraternal. Islam inspires the family to be closely knit by the power of mutual attachment, the only permanent link possible. The fire of passion (lust) is, on the contrary, a killer that causes jealousy and possessiveness. If a family catches such a fire, brothers may kill one another in rivalry over a beautiful sister; the family would be doomed, having exploded from within.

God commands us to keep away only from things that are better avoided. He commands people to have what is genuinely worth having. Divorce, though necessary when an actual breakdown of marriage occurs, is not a practice that God commends, but allows.

Lying is the most odious of all cardinal sins.

> *O ye who believe!*
> *Why say ye that*
> *Which ye do not?*
> *(The Battle Array, 61: 3)*

To lie is to commit a heinous sin.

> *Who doth more wrong*
> *Than he who inventeth*
> *A lie against Allah*
> *Or rejecteth His Signs?*
> *(The Cattle, 6: 21)*

To assert falsely that one is a prophet, to tamper with the holy Scriptures, to claim that certain verses are revealed when they are a forgery is quite unlawful because it does harm and misleads people.

Such is Islamic Law, and such its spirit! God has ordained all good things lawful and all bad things unlawful. Pure hearts will easily love the things decreed by God. There can be, therefore, no contradiction in a believer's heart between God and His Law on the one hand and what he, as an individual, aspires to, on the other. The two lines always converge, what a man wants and what God wants him to have; what he hopes for and what God hopes him to have. Listen to Abraham's supplication:

> O my Lord! make me
> One who establishes regular Prayers
> (The Prophet Abraham [Ibrahim], 14: 40)

Abraham is asking God for what God is asking him to do, an expression of the deepest possible faith and trust in God's law. Here divine command and individual desire ultimately coalesce, as man wants nothing beyond what God wants him to have. People who have "arrived," to use a popular term must feel this way. In a *Qudsi hadith*, God says:

> "O My servant, if you are obedient, I
> will make you Godly: your hand will be
> as My hand, your tongue as My tongue,
> your sight as My sight, your will as My
> will, your desire as My desire."

A high rank is reserved for those who are near to God – prophets, saints and good people – who are provided with God's own knowledge and power.

Chapter 6
Knowledge and Action

The first word of the Qur'an revealed to the Prophet was *Read*.

Proclaim! (or Read!)
In the name of thy Lord and Cherisher,
Who created –
(The Clinging Clot [or Read], 96: 1)

It was the first divine command in Islam. Every man should read. Before ordaining prayers and fasting, before giving details of the creed and the law to be revealed, God said, "Read!" The Qur'an is the only holy book that opens with this word and command. It is a great honor to knowledge and to the learned that the first word in our religion should be a command to read and acquire knowledge. The verse specifies the kind of knowledge to be acquired initially:

Read!

In the name of thy Lord who has created – a knowledge of God, useful and virtuous knowledge. Subsequently, verses were revealed (so many in fact) which command and urge people to acquire knowledge.

"O my Lord, advance me in knowledge."
(Ta Ha, 20: 114)

Say: Travel through the earth
And see how Allah did
Originate creation, then
Repeats it: truly that
Is easy for Allah
(The Spider, 29: 20)

Allah will raise up, to (suitable) ranks
(And degrees), those of you
Who believe and who been granted knowledge.
(The Woman Who Pleads, 58: 11)

Say, 'Are those equal, those who know
And those who do not know?
(Crowds, 39: 9)

There is no god but He
That is the witness of Allah,
His angels, and those endued
With knowledge, standing firm
(The Family of 'Imran, 3: 18)

In the last verse, God places the learned by his side, along with the angels, as far as the value of their testimony is concerned, which is the highest rank possible. The Arabic word for knowledge and its derivatives occur about 850 times in the Qur'an. God vows by the pen:

'Nuun'
By the Pen
And by the (Record)
Which men (write) –
(The Pen, 68: 1)

It is not, however, only theoretical knowledge that is meant;

the Qur'an means all knowledge to lead to action.

Say, 'Work; (righteousness):
Soon Allah will observe your work
(Repentance, 9: 105)

Wherever the Qur'an mentions the believers, their faith is made to lead to or is associated with work. "Those who believe and work righteous deeds" is a commonly occurring phrase in the Qur'an. The recurrence of such a combination as faith and work is meant to impress on our minds that no faith can be correct unless combined with work. It is the deeds that reveal intentions of virtue, charity, and obedience.

Because the first command in the Qur'an concerns reading and learning (nothing can be more explicit in fact), no ignorant person should claim to be a Muslim even though he prays, fasts, and plays about with the beads in his rosary all day. The ignorance and idleness on the rampage today in the Muslim World indicates that we do not believe in the essential teachings of our book; instead of learning and work, there is ignorance and laziness. Ironically, everyone thinks that he's going to Heaven simply because he happens to be a Muslim by birth and owns a copy of the Qur'an! He never considers the fact that although the first word revealed in that Qur'an was "*Read*," and that God consistently commands us to work, he neither reads nor works, preferring to kill his time yawning at cafes. Indeed, it is the Western nations today who are showing such an interest in learning, working, continuous creativity, and intellectual activity that are nearer to the essence of Islam than the lazy and idle East, sinking as it does in a pool of ignoble ignorance.

Shouldn't we understand the Qur'an before claiming that we belong to the Qur'an? Some Muslims blame their laziness and ignorance on mysticism. They believe that, once in seclusion to meditate on nothing they have earned the title of mystics. Shouldn't they too know that a mystic's real journey to God must start with learning and end up with working? A real mystic should learn first, then proceed to apply his knowledge to life; having enough good works to his credit, his station invariably changes and in time his rank in the eyes of God improves. The hard work of a mystic is the essential link between learning and the changed position to which he aspires. He proceeds, to put it succinctly, from learning to working, thence to a higher station, and ultimately to a lofty rank. The early mystics were soldiers who defended their land, venturing forth with a copy of the Qur'an in one hand and a sword in the other. In North Africa, you can visit some of the innumerable tombs of those murabitin. The Arabic word *murabit*, which today generally indicates a mystic, really means a soldier who was tied down to his position, having been immolated in his devotional defense of his home (from *Rabata* = to tie, or bind.)

Courage, gallantry, truthfulness; to fight against wrong, in defense of right; to work for the prosperity of the world by vindicating benevolence and justice, fighting exploitation, and supporting the weak and meek – all are qualities and deeds essential to our religion, if they do not constitute our religion itself. If you don't take part in them, you'll not be a true believer, nor will you belong to the Qur'an.

Before taking any action, however, there should be knowledge. Read first; be able to distinguish right from wrong, and know the laws of the world in which you live, before you can claim that you can reform that world. Careful to show us the way, rather than leave us to wild guessing, the Qur'an establishes a method, namely, to move and examine.

*Say, 'Journey in the land, and behold
how He originated creation,'*

To move, to marshal observations, to record data, then to examine all available facts in order to establish the general law that governs them is the method of induction instituted by Bacon a thousand years after the Qur'an was revealed. It was this method that helped Western scientists to make great advances in science and technology, to establish the ever-expanding base of modern industry. If we had made an effort to understand our Book and act according to its commands, we should have beaten them to those modern sciences.

A few Arab scientists had in fact discovered that method in the early days of Islam. Their contribution to human knowledge enriched the Western culture at a time when the whole of Europe had been plunged into the ignorance of the Dark Ages. We remember the pioneers such as Jabir Ibn Hayyan, in chemistry; Ibn Arabi, in mysticism; and Ibn Haytham, in mathematics and geometry. We remember the innovations of the Andalusian poets and musicians. We have heard of the Arab astronomers; in fact most constellations still keep their Arabic names in foreign books. The words used by Jabir Ibn Hayyan for the distilling apparatus he had invented, namely *Anbeeq*, is still used in French, viz., *Ambique*, hence the French verb *ambiquer*, i.e., to distill. The decimal system in mathematics was invented by the Arabs and thence transferred to Europe.

Our ancestors combined their knowledge with work, and the combination made a vast contribution to the march of civilization, the key for which being provided by the Qur'an, *Read*. It was this key, the first word revealed, that Muhammad was commanded to convey to his nation. He who does not read, therefore, is not worthy to belong to Muhammad's nation, nor can he claim to know the Qur'an; and he who has knowledge but does not employ it, will be inactive, ineffectual and unreligious. The Qur'an describes Abraham's building of the House of God:

> And remember Abraham
> And Isma'il raised
> The foundations of the House
> (with this prayer): "Our Lord!
> Accept (this service) from us:
> For thou are the All-Hearing,
> The All-Knowing."
> (The Heifer, 2: 127)

The mind is the architect, the hand is the work, while the heart sings the glories of God, whispering the prayer: Our Lord! Accept this service from us; Thou art the All-Hearing, the All-Knowing. The act combined knowledge and work; faith and construction. Such is the true religion as presented by the Qur'an. In fact, the Qur'an has the best things to say about working believers:

> Those who have faith
> And do righteous deeds—
> They are the best of creatures
> (The Clear Evidence, 98: 7)

> And who speaks fairer than he who
> Calls unto God and does righteousness.
> (Expounded, 41: 33)

It is stressed that all our deeds are recorded and that God will present us with the record thereof on the Day of Reckoning:

And whatever
Deed ye (mankind) may be doing,
We are Witnesses thereof
(The Prophet Jonah [Yunus], 10: 61)

On the day when every soul
Will be confronted
With all the good it has done,
And all the evil it has done,
It will wish there were
A great distance
Between it and its evil.
(The Family of 'Imran, 3: 30)

Thus will Allah show them
(The fruits of) their deeds
As (nothing but) regrets
(The Heifer, 2: 167)

They will find all that they did
Placed before them:
And not one will thy Lord
Treat with injustice.
(The Cave, 18: 49)

The Qur'an emphasizes that this world presents the only chance for good deeds. It is the only test allowed. Of the people in Hell, it says:

Therein will they cry
Aloud (for assistance):
"Our Lord! Bring us out:
We shall work righteousness,
Not the (deeds) we used to do!"
(The Originator of Creation, 35: 37)

But it would be too late, of course.

> But if they were returned,
> They would certainly relapse
> To the things they were forbidden,
> For indeed they are liars.
> (The Cattle, 6: 28)

It is all over; no excuse accepted.

The Qur'an stresses that good works done not out of faith cannot be regarded as good works; such good works by a man whose heart denies its own Creator will be futile.

> And we shall turn to whatever deeds
> They did [in this life] and we shall make
> Such deeds as floating dust scattered about.
> (The Criterion, 25: 23)

> The parable of those who
> Reject their Lord is that
> Their works are as ashes,
> On which the wind blows
> Furiously on a tempestuous day
> (The Prophet Abraham [Ibrahim], 14: 18)

A question may be raised: How can a good deed be deprived of goodness if the heart of the doer is lacking in faith? If an atheist makes a donation to charity, wouldn't it be good work for which he deserves recompense? The answer is easy: An infidel – that is, a person who does not believe in God – will believe all work to originate in himself. He would think that it is he who contributes and donates; and if he is responsible for people's livelihood, he could cause them to be rich or poor. Such a belief is based on vanity and pride. It cannot therefore qualify any work to be acceptable as good. When on the other hand, a believer makes a donation, he must believe that he is no more than an instrument of God's Will, that God has inspired him to subscribe to charity, having first given him money, a kind heart, and a disposition to generosity. Made in humility, such a donation would indeed be "good."

The Qur'an stresses that a will to do good work, without actually doing it, is not enough to prove a man's faith. A desire to fight in the cause of God is not enough; a man must actually fight; he must confront death and prove his fortitude.

> Did ye *think that ye would enter Heaven*
> *Without Allah's testing those of you who*
> *Fought hard (in His cause) and remained steadfast?*
> *(The Family of 'Imran, 3: 142)*

A will that does not take the shape of action must be less than genuine. It may be more of a feigned than a real desire, because only genuine desires lead to action. God tells us, in fact, that he created this world for this reason.

> *He who created Death and Life, that He*
> *May try which of you is best in deed*
> *(The Dominion, 67: 2)*

The world is a test of deeds; and the result of the test will establish the ranks of every human being. Once judgment is established, there cannot be any change or tampering with the result. The verdict passed on the Day of Judgment will thus be based on ultimate and absolute justice, being accounted for in terms of concrete deeds. The Qur'an says:

O ye who believe!
Do your duty to Allah,
Seek the means
Of approach unto Him
(The Repast, 5: 35)

The "means" is, of course, work.

Our Prophet Muhammad, the example we should follow, was not merely a man who conveyed the Message to his people, or simply served as a reciter of the Qur'an to warn and admonish. He was a hard worker. He was the first to rush forth in times of wars; he led his army on the battlefield and shared the life of his soldiers, their hunger, and their thirst. He was the first to brave dangers. We know that he was once wounded in one of his battles, one of the twenty-seven he fought (though he was over fifty years of age.) He was a prophet who conveyed a message, a soldier who fought his battles, a commander who planned both strategy and tactics, and a politician who administered the affairs of state with prudence. Apart from this, he was a devout, unworldly worshipper, truthful and honest, never sullying his hand or his tongue. He was a kind father, a good husband and a faithful friend, even while the call to Islam was his permanent preoccupation. We know that he never shirked a burden in the service of that cause for which he fought and for which he would have died.

He is the epitome of incessant work. He is the example to follow, if you seek to reach the right destination. You can't get there except through work. The only journey to God is upwards on the stairway of good deeds.

Chapter 7

The Names of God

I t is impossible to know anything about the real entity of God. It is impossible for a human eye to see Him because it can only perceive something that is finite in space and time. God, however, is transcendent, and infinite both spatially and temporally; there is nothing like Him. In beautifully rhythmical verses, the Qur'an expresses this eternal truth:

He knoweth the Unseen
And that which is open:
He is the Great,
The Most High.
(The Thunder, 13: 9)

Who (dare to) dispute
About Allah with the strength
Of his power (supreme)!
(The Thunder, 13: 13)

With Him are the keys of the Unseen;
The treasures that none knoweth but He.
He knoweth whatever there is
On the earth and in the sea
(The Cattle, 6: 59)

Whatever beings there are
In the heavens and the earth
Do prostrate themselves to Allah
(The Thunder, 13: 15)

All prostrations are due to God alone. Any being that doesn't prostrate willingly, does so unwillingly because all must obey the natural laws of God, laws that He has established. The heart of the infidel, no less than that of the believer, is governed by the physiological laws established by the Creator because both hearts beat in accordance with the same laws, as well as every cell in every living body. Hence the following verse:

> *Do they seek for other than the Religion of Allah? –*
> *While all creatures in the heavens and on earth*
> *Have willingly or unwillingly,*
> *Bowed to His Will (accepted Islam),*
> *And to Him shall they all be brought back.*
> *(The Family of 'Imran, 3: 83)*

All beings have surrendered to the divine laws governing life. We today know many of these laws: osmotic pressure; surface tension; the cohesion of the water column; electric and ionic balance in solutions; and the chemical preferential law which determines the supremacy of one hormone over another; vacuum rejection; action and reaction. God and his laws govern and maintain the existence of all beings, from the atom to the vast cosmos. He is the Living and the *Qayyoum*, that is, He is self-subsisting and He keeps up and maintains all life. The Qur'an presents the names, the attributes, and the deeds of God in beautiful songs of glory:

> *Allah is He, than Whom there is no other god–*
> *The Sovereign, the Holy One,*
> *The Source of Peace (and Perfection),*
> *The Guardian of Faith,*
> *The Preserver of Safety,*
> *the Exalted in Might,*
> *The Irresistible, the Supreme*
> *(The Mustering, 59: 23)*

He is Allah, the Creator, the Evolver,
The Bestower of Forms [or colors]
(The Mustering, 59: 24)

Of Himself He uses a plural personal pronoun:

We are nearer to him than the jugular vein
(Qaf, 50: 16)

The jugular vein is in the neck, which means that God is nearer to us than the blood in our own bodies, which is very near indeed!

Mystics say that Allah is difficult to perceive because He happens to be too near, that He is concealed from us because He is too obvious. We have known sunlight, they explain, because it disappears; we can recognize the colors of things because of the light falling on them, (though we cannot know the essence of these things); we know that they are blue, red or green, because they absorb different wavelengths of light. Shade helps us to know light. But Allah has no antithesis to help us understand what He is because Allah's light is always shining, everlastingly, without any possibility of shadows. That is why we say that Allah is concealed from our sight because He is too bright and permanent.

Born in the presence of Allah, we begin by having limited rational faculties. As we grow up, we are diverted from the divine presence by our growing reason and physical desires. Preoccupied at a later stage with worldly affairs, with worldly eminence and power, we reach maturity only to be diverted once more by so-called mature reasoning. Throughout these stages, the original feeling of divine presence becomes taken for granted, and the marvels of Allah's creation in the heavens, on the earth and in ourselves become a matter of course, we simply get used to them and fail to be conscious of them. A mystic poet sums it all up in one line:

Too well known to be known; too obvious to be seen!

In other words, we are too absorbed in examining the phenomena to recognize the phenomenon. It is as though one has received a book but instead of reading it, one focuses on the kind of ink used, the paper, or the printer's type. Indeed, one may read the book but forget that it ever had an author! Permanence blinds us to existence: we tend to be unaware of that which is permanently present: we are likely to be unconscious of the elevator's movement until it has stopped. The fact that Allah is permanent, continuously present with us, makes us unaware of His presence; being too near makes Him difficult to perceive; being too obvious makes Him impossible to see. He is the most concealed because He is the most conspicuous.

The only veil between man and Allah is that of man's own senses, the thick veil of physical desires which blocks our vision. However, Allah can never be veiled; as Ibn 'Ata-Allah al-Sakandari says:

If a veil does exist, it would indeed hide Him; but if anything hides Him, He would be finite; Glory be to God and hallowed be His Name! How can the infinite be finite?

One cannot see the pupil of one's eye because it is too near!

To the mystics Allah's existence needs no proof. It is the world that is called in question and requires a proof. They adduce the presence of Allah as proof of the world's existence, not the other way round. Only those whose eyes are veiled may require proof of Allah's existence, those who see the Creation but not the Creator.

Al-Sakandari wonders:

Was God ever inconspicuous to require signs of
His existence? Was He ever so far away to make
worldly phenomena a means of reaching Him?

Mystics are driven by love towards Allah, not because they are afraid of Hell fire or ambitious to go to Paradise. They say they are on a constant journey to God – from the universe to the universe-maker. This is a different kind of journey. On earth one leaves one spot for another, only to return to the original spot. An earthly journey for them is a circling round, more like that of an animal moving a grindstone. But the journey mystics have in mind is a movement from the physical to the spiritual kingdom, from the world of the senses to the world of meaning.

Mystics are odd sometimes. They have interesting views that often prove profound enough. They say that sometimes an act of disobedience to God could in reality be better than one of obedience. An offense could on occasion make one afraid of God's might; it could teach you humility and submission. On the other hand, an act of piety may in effect make you feel proud and vain. A wrongdoer will thus be nearer to God and will have more humility than the pious. An act of piety, they explain, may make a man proud; a man may feel gratified with what is commonly regarded as good work; but the fact that he is conscious of this work, let alone being pleased with it, will make it valueless as good work.

Good works ascend to God the minute they are done, even before their author is conscious of them. Mystics believe that a genuinely good man is never conscious of his good work; he is, on the contrary, conscious only of his trepidation in the presence of God. This is, in fact, their interpretation of the following verse:

> *To Him mount up (all) Words of Purity:*
> *It is He Who exalts each deed of righteousness*
> *(The Originator of Creation, 35: 10)*

According to them, thanksgiving does not consist in saying, "Thanks be to the Lord." To be truly thankful is to obey your benefactor. Obedience puts God's gifts to good use, preventing them from doing harm to their authors and other people. Thanksgiving should be in deed rather than in words.

The mystic, the yogi and the monk are all trying to reach God, though taking different paths. They all believe that physical desire veils one's perception, just like a soul's vain passions or love of this world. Even knowledge can turn into a very thick veil indeed if a man takes pride in it. If worship becomes a source of vanity, it will trick the worshipper; and the same applies to good deeds. Consider the following verse:

> *And they say: "What sort of a messenger is this*
> *Who eats food and walks through the streets?"*
> *(The Criterion, 25: 7)*

According to the learned opinions of the commentators, the meaning is that God has provided the prophet with human apparel so as to protect the divine mystery from being disclosed. In other words, the prophet should appear as a common man who walks and eats like all others.

The yogi, the monk, and the Muslim mystic all seek to reach God by reciting His names, by singing songs of praise, and by piety, worship and good works. They call on God by repeating His names:

The Most Beautiful Names
Belong to Allah;
So call on Him by them
(The Heights, 7: 180)

There is a special yoga exercise concerned with the songs of praise, called *Mantrayoga*, which comes from the Sanskrit word for incantation *Mantram* (cf. Sanskrit *mantar* = thinker). One of the most common incantations is the repetition of the words *Raheem, Rehaam* thousands of times (equivalent to Arabic *Raheem, Rahmaan*), which are two of God's names in Sanskrit. Around his neck, the Yogi wears long strings, consisting of a thousand beads each.

Islam offers man the shortest and safest path to God. The Qur'an being the only holy book that has not been tampered with or corrupted in any way. Al-Ghazali believes that Islamic incantation is at its purest when performed in silence, by the heart. In solitude and perfect stillness the spirit reads out the names of God, without the mouth uttering a word:

Bring thy Lord to remembrance
In thy (very) soul,
With humility and in reverence,
Without loudness in words.
(The Heights, 7: 205)

This is the highest rank in mysticism. It can only be attained by those who have serenity of soul, purity of heart, and, most important, the capacity for full concentration and the will power needed to defeat mundane interests and desires. Only those could hope to mount the path to God, more difficult than flying to the moon because it involves a huge effort of the will against the soul's base desires.

For the would-be mystic, the first step would be to defeat himself. The self is a veil, much as the mind and social conventions are. They represent a person's psychological skin — the walls inevitably erected around him or her. If he can get over them, he will be able to perceive his spirit in its virginal state; he will see what no human eye has ever seen, and hear what no human ear has ever heard.

Mysticism is therefore a method of perception with the higher faculties of the human spirit. The mystic is a learned man; his learning is designed to make possible communion with the perfection of God rather than the accumulation of such imperfect pieces of information as are provided by the earthly disciplines of physics and chemistry, or geography and history. He seeks to attain a kind of comprehensive and wholistic knowledge using difficult faculties; and his instruments are therefore different from those used in positivist science and logic. This explains why the steep path is regarded by the mystic as his own self.

> But he hath made no haste
> On the path that is steep;
> And what will explain
> To thee the path that is steep?
> (The City, 90: 11-12)

Prophet David once asked God where he could find Him. God's reply was, "Leave thyself and come; separate from thyself and thou wilt find Me." Following this line of argument, some mystics have ventured an allegorical interpretation of God's command to Moses:

> Put off thy shoes; thou art
> In the sacred valley Tuwa.
> (Ta Ha, 20: 12)

They assert that the two shoes are meant to refer to the soul and the body, the soul's desires and the body's pleasures. No person can hope to meet God until he (or she) has removed these two, the soul and the body, either by death or by mortification. They are compared to the shoes because they resemble the two feet with which the spirit wades in the morass of the material world. They were the cause of the spirit's fall from its original heavens to the earth.

You may object to the allegorical interpretation, believing the literal meaning to be adequate. But the former is necessary because no one can gain admittance to God's presence merely by taking off his shoes. He must remove, in fact, all the trappings of the physical world, particularly the mundane preoccupations that weigh down both soul and body. The mystical meaning is there, no doubt, and the verse must be interpreted in this way as well. But this interpretation is not contradictory with the literal meaning of the words. It is natural for a mystic to remove those symbolic shoes before taking his first steps into the holy valley.

That we shall be in God's presence after resurrection is made amply clear:

> *And fear Allah,*
> *And know that ye are*
> *To meet Him (in the Hereafter)*
> *(The Heifer, 2: 223)*

> *Every one of them*
> *Will come to Him singly*
> *On the day of Judgement*
> *(Mary, 19: 95)*

> *O thou man! Verily thou art ever toiling*
> *on towards thy Lord – Painfully toiling –*
> *But thou shalt meet Him.*
> *(The Rending Asunder, 84: 6)*

And behold! ye come
To Us bare and alone
As We created you
For the first time.
(The Cattle, 6: 94)

And thy Lord cometh,
and His angels rank upon rank
(The Dawn, 89: 22)

(All) faces will be humbled
Before (Him) – the Living,
The Self-Subsisting, Eternal:
Hopeless indeed will be
The man that carries
Iniquity (on his back)
(Ta Ha, 20: 111)

If only thou couldst see
When the guilty ones
Will bend low their heads
Before their Lord
(The Prostration, 32: 12)

Their salutation on the Day
They meet Him will be
"Peace!": and He has
Prepared for them a generous Reward.
(The Confederates, 33: 44)

One day will Allah raise them all up
(For Judgement): then will they swear to Him
As they swear to you:, and they think that they
Have something (to stand upon).
No indeed! they are but liars.
(The Plea of a Woman, 58: 18)

Will they wait until Allah comes to them
In canopies of clouds, with angels (in His train)
And the question is (thus) settled?
(The Heifer, 2: 210)

Some Muslim sects argue that it is impossible to see God in the other world, opting for an allegorical interpretation of these verses. Their argument rests briefly on the fact that the human eye can only perceive that which is finite, temporally and spatially, while God is infinite and transcendent to both time and space. This is, I believe, a flimsy argument because it is based on materialistic, worldly assumptions, most important of which is that the spirit will use the physical eye in perception in the after-life, that this eye will have a pupil and lids and so will be governed by the limitations of earthly time and space. The Qur'an refutes this, however, by stating that God will cause us to rise again in different forms, forms that are completely unknown to us:

From changing your Forms
And creating you (again)
In (Forms) that ye know not.
(The Inevitable, 56: 61)

Would it be surprising at all if God granted our spirits the power to see the infinite (to conceive if not perceive it) and so see God in the other world?

Now the Qur'an reveals to us ninety-nine of the beautiful names of Allah. Some of these pertain to God alone, such as Allah, while others are attributes of His, such as *Kareem* (generous), *Haleem* (forbearing), *Raouf* (kind), *Wadood* (loving), etc. The latter category may be used as names for men, while *Allah* is naturally reserved for Allah. The quiddity of Allah is an inscrutable mystery that no human mind should ever approach, while the other attributes may be pondered at will.

> And your Lord says:
> "Call on Me; I will answer your (Prayer)"
> (Forgiver / The Believer, 40: 60)

> When My servants
> Ask thee concerning Me,
> I am indeed close (to them): I listen
> To the prayer of every
> Suppliant when he calleth on Me.
> (The Heifer, 2: 186)

This is true of course; however, the call to God does not consist in only uttering such words as "My God!" Any man can cry out "O God!" without being conscious of the meaning of the words. The call to God is in fact a most serious thing to do; it pertains to, if it is not, mysticism itself. Only men of lofty hearts, profound insight and great will power are capable of it. This does not mean that you must be a dervish before you can expect God to answer your call. On the contrary, any person can expect it if he or she is pure of heart and, which is equally important, if he or she addresses God with an undivided sense of allegiance.

He who says, "O God, grant me a hundred dollars!" makes an absurd joke. Moneymaking has its well-known worldly methods, but mysticism is not one of them; a small tobacco shop on the street corner will do the trick! On the other hand, a mystic could never seek such material gains, because he sets himself a higher goal. Indeed, a mystic finds it difficult, out of decency, to ask even for better health; if unwell, he would still be shy to call to God for recovery. "How could I presume," he would say, "to have a will of my own which may be contrary to God's will? How could I ask

Him to do something that He might not have originally wanted to do? I do not even know what is good for me or what is bad! How can the ignorant object to the knowledgeable? How do I know that my pains do not constitute the means of my redemption?"

This is carrying the matter too far, of course, and the Muslim is not expected to be an extremist. In fact, as the previous verses make clear, God likes our calling to Him. It is just that the mystic would like to have his own and God's will concur and out of fear and humility, he would ask God for only that which God asks of him. He would ideally stick to the Abrahamic formula:

> O my Lord! make me
> One who establishes regular Prayer,
> And also (raise such)
> Among my offspring
> O our Lord!
> And accept Thou my Prayer.
> (The Prophet Abraham [Ibrahim], 14: 40)

That is, to adopt God's will as his own — out of love and respect for his Creator. Love is the highest object of the mystic. He would remind that God says:

> I have only created Jinn and men, that
> They may serve Me
> (The Winds That Scatter, 51: 56)

This means that God created the jinn and humankind to know Him, as it is impossible to serve someone unknown. There cannot be worship without knowledge. And the first step toward knowledge of God is to know oneself. Self-knowledge will help a person transcend the self in search of the Creator of that self. Mystically interpreted, the verse implies all such steps of knowledge. Man was created to know himself or herself first then know his/her God. Only thus can there be hope to gain clarity of vision and actual ascendance through the conflict of body and soul.

This kind of ascendance is achieved also through integration following a bloody battle between the dust-created body and the spirit.

> *Verily We have created*
> *Man into toil and struggle*
> *(The City, 90: 4)*

Mankind was created to fight that battle, and those who win are promised the inheritance of earth and heaven.

To serve the Creator, even as a slave, is to enjoy full freedom among God's creatures; to be humbled down to the Creator is to hold your head high among all other beings. For serving God means primarily your freedom from worldly bonds, from being a slave to money, your desires, worldly eminence, and ambition. He who worships God cannot worship the applause of the mob or pander to popular demands. In other words, you cannot be truly a servant of God until you have succeeded in breaking the chains of these mundane masters. Once you do so, your heart will then be free to worship God and God alone.

You cannot, in fact, reach the topmost rung in the ladder of worship until you have succeeded in mortifying your self and your desires, so that whatever you want for yourself will be the same as what God wants for you. Your will must then concur with God's, and, having cast away all forms of servitude, you will attain ultimate freedom.

The mystic is a man of thought and meditation; he is extraordinarily sensitive and has profound insight. A typical mystical saying is:

Your only genuine friend is He who,
notwithstanding the flaws in your
character, maintains your friendship;

He is your God, your Creator, who
knows you inside out; He knows what
you hide and what you reveal. If you
disobey Him, He would still shelter you;
if you apologize to Him, He would
accept your apology.

If you have a little to be joyful about,
You will have as little to be sad about.

If you are loath to be removed from
office, do not accept temporary posts.

If you claim to be modest, you are
verily proud.

If you recognize God only in His blessings,
you will be worshipping yourself, not God.

God created the world to put it in your
service, but you now serve it; He wanted
you to be a king, but you want to be a slave.

The mystic would thus address the theologians:

You have acquired your knowledge by
copying the ideas of the dead; but we
receive knowledge from the living God.
You refer to dead scholars while the
real source of knowledge is always with
you – nearer to you than your jugular vein.
He is omnipresent; why leave Him
and seek knowledge elsewhere?

That is why Muslim mystics describe their knowledge as *ladunni*, that is,"from God," not copied from books. They describe themselves as the people of the Divine Presence. They undertake serious spiritual exercising, fasting, and praying to the point of complete mortification. Their means of reaching God is the recitation of His beautiful names and overflowing love for Him. They think of nothing else. There is nothing they see, but they see God therein.

These are the "Beholders of the Mystery," witnesses of divine power, and nearest to God. They are saintly and truly good people, but they are rare indeed and difficult to discover. You could be with them but fail to recognize them for they never reveal themselves. A genuine mystic conceals his (or her) God-granted power as zealously as he covers his genitals; it is the secret bond he has with God, the sign of love and proximity.

However, these must not be confused with the self-proclaimed dervishes on the streets, the beggars who litter the mosques, loquacious quacks, impostors, or professional faith-healers. Mystics are secretly pious. In a *Qudsi* hadith, Allah says:

> My intimate seekers live under My domes;
> They are known only to Me.

Concerning the private relationship He has with them, God says in another *Qudsi hadith*:

> My Earth and My Heaven are not vast enough for Me;
> The heart of my faithful servant is.

In another *Qudsi hadith*, He says:

> O My servant if you are obedient,
> I will make you Godly:

Your hand will be as My hand,
your tongue as My tongue,
Your sight as My sight.

How rare these days such Godly people are!

Chapter 8

One God, One Religion

In unequivocal verses, the Qur'an states decisively and in precise terms that there is no god but God, that nothing truly exists but He, that everything else is vain and ephemeral. Revelation comes to Muhammad to state in definite terms:

> *Know, therefore, that there is no god*
> *But Allah, and ask forgiveness for thy fault*
> *(Muhammad, 47: 19)*

> *Everything (that exists) will perish*
> *Except His own Face*
> *(The Narrations, 28: 88)*

Christ says in the Gospel, "Do not call a (holy) father for you on earth, for your Father is One, your Lord that is in Heaven." He also says, "Go hence, Satan! It is preordained that thou should bow down to the Lord, your God, and Him alone worship." The Torah has words to the same effect. The Torah, in fact, describes God as one, unincarnate, who neither eats nor suffers any imperfections. All Holy Scriptures — the Torah, the Gospel, and the Qur'an — are, as revealed, monotheistic books commanding faith in one God.

The Qur'an states clearly and unequivocally that all "people of the Book," that is both Jews and Christians, before the revelation of the Qur'an to Muhammad, would actually be following the right path if they adhered to monotheism, and that they would be fairly recompensed in the other world. The Qur'an further states that even those who had directed their faces to the sun as a symbol of God's power, that is, the Sabians, such as the ancient Egyptian king Akhenaton, were religious to their own day and would be rewarded. The same applies to the Jews before the advent of Christianity, and to the Christians before Islam: all will enjoy forgiveness and have their wages.

> Those who believe (in the Qur' an),
> And those who follow the Jewish (Scriptures),
> And the Christians and the Sabians —
> Any who believe in Allah
> And the Last Day,
> And work righteousness,
> Shall have their reward
> With their Lord; on them
> Shall be no fear, nor shall they grieve.
> (The Heifer, 2: 62)

The Qur'an tells us that to imagine that true religions are contradictory is to betray crass ignorance:

> The Jews say: "The Christians
> Have naught (to stand) upon";
> And the Christians say:
> "The Jews have naught
> (To stand) upon." Yet they
> (Profess to) study the (same) Book.
> Like unto their word
> Is what those say who know not;
> But Allah will judge
> Between them in their quarrel
> On the Day of Judgement.
> (The Heifer, 2: 113)

Those who differ over this do not understand the reality of religion; for in reality, all religion is one:

> *The same religion has He established*
> *Which He enjoined on Noah –*
> *That which We have sent*
> *By inspiration to thee –*
> *And that We enjoined on Abraham, Moses and Jesus;*
> *Namely, that ye should remain*
> *Steadfast in Religion, and make*
> *No divisions therein*
> *(Consultation, 42: 13)*

Where *belief* is concerned, it is definitely one religion. The laws instituted by that religion were, however, revealed by stages. Any apparent differences between scripture-based religions are in fact due to the differences between laws.

> *To each among you*
> *Have We prescribed*
> *A Law and an Open Way.*
> *(The Repast, 5: 48)*

Christ says that his task was not to contradict divine law but to complement it. What we have here is, therefore, a process, or an advance in stages. As the human soul advances to maturity, God appoints the right prophet and reveals to him the right law, that is, the most suitable for that particular stage. Further advance by mankind will require, however, more change and so more prophets are appointed to "complement" the law, that is, to make it capable of keeping abreast of man's spiritual development.

In the time of Moses, the age of the Pharaohs, when power and violence reigned supreme, the law of justice was revealed to Moses.

And the right kind of justice for that age was equal retaliation, an eye for an eye and a tooth for a tooth (in other words, let the punishment fit the crime). But as man advanced, the law of love was prescribed. Most memorable are Christ's words in the Gospel about turning the left cheek too. Such a lofty code of ethics, however, could not survive, the tyranny of the despots and the proud man's insolence. Christ and the Christians were persecuted, hanged, and burned at the stake. Love was put to the hardest and worst ever test. The mighty tyrants considered Christian love a weakness and exploited it in crushing the advocates of love.

The Islamic law had to be revealed, combining the law of justice and the law of love. The new law may be rightly described as the law of mercy. The Qur'an says:

> And if ye do punish them,
> Punish them no worse
> Than they afflicted you:
> But if ye show patience,
> That is indeed the best (course)
> For those who are patient.
> And do thou be patient,
> For thy patience is but
> From Allah; nor grieve over them:
> And distress not thyself
> Because of their plots.
> (The Bee, 16: 126-127)

The Qur'an thus makes it legitimate to defend oneself by force (when the Gospel had forbidden it) so as to prevent the tyrannical from exploiting the weakness of the faithful, and to support "Right" with the necessary physical power in the future.

God knew that a time would come when only the logic of force would reign and only the powerful would dominate.

Though self-defense is legitimate, patience is to be preferred; forbearance is better. And the verse concludes with the direct command: "Do thou be patient, for thy patience is but from God." God promises, in other words, to help the faithful in showing patience. Furthermore, the Qur'an is quite explicit in tipping the balance in favor of love by advising the believers to reply to evil by doing good. The relevant command is precise:

> Repel evil with that which is best.
>
> (The Believers, 23: 96)

Such a careful and delicately balanced combination of justice and love, within the wider framework of mercy and kindness, has been the right combination for man and will be so for the remainder of his life on earth.

God knows that man will undergo no further spiritual change, that he will succeed only in developing and improving his tools — making motorcars, trains, aircraft, and rockets. Man may succeed in conquering fresh fields of science and rationalist philosophy, but he will definitely fail to make any comparable advance in his spiritual constitution. Consequently, Muhammad became the last of God's prophets; there was nothing more to say where the spiritual life of man was concerned. It is still our duty, I believe, to inquire into what has been said, and why God's messengers no longer come to tell us any more.

Religion is therefore One, and God is One.

Those who differed over this failed to grasp the fact that the Tablets, the Ten Commandments, and other revealed laws were designed to match the development of the human spirit.

God explains the matter further in the Qur'an, stating with the utmost precision that all prophets, separated as they were by great intervals, were actually the messengers of one Religion. He refers to them as Muslims and to their religion as Islam. Noah thus addresses the unbelievers:

> My reward is only due from Allah,
> And I have been commanded to be
> Of those who submit to Allah's Will in Islam
> (The Prophet Jonah [Yunus], 10: 72)

The Qur'an uses the same term with reference to Abraham and his sons (when building the Ka'ba)

> And remember Abraham
> And Isma'il raised
> The foundations of the House
> (With this prayer): "Our Lord!
> Accept (this service) from us:
> For Thou art the All-Hearing,
> The All-Knowing.
> "Our Lord! make of us
> Muslims, bowing to Thy (Will),
> And of our progeny a people
> Muslim, bowing to Thy (Will),
> And show us our places for
> The celebration of (due) rites;
> And turn unto us (in Mercy);
> For Thou art the Oft-Returning,
> Most Merciful.
> (The Heifer, 2: 127-128)

And Moses too:

Moses said: "O my people!
If you do (really) believe in Allah,
Then in Him put your trust
If ye submit (your will to His)."
(The Prophet Jonah [Yunus], 10: 84)

Overwhelmed by the rising water, and about to die, Pharaoh said:

"I believe that there is no god
Except in Whom the Children
Of Israel believe:
I am of those who submit
(To Allah in Islam)."
(The Prophet Jonah [Yunus], 10: 90)

Reunited with his family, Joseph had the following to say:

"O my Lord! Thou hast
Indeed bestowed on me
Some power, and taught me
Something of the interpretation
Of dreams and events – O Thou
Creator of the heavens
And the earth! Thou art
My Protector in this world
And in the Hereafter.
Take Thou my soul (at death)
As one submitting to Thy will
(As a Muslim), and unite me
With the righteous."
(The Prophet Joseph [Yusuf], 12: 101)

The Egyptian magicians who believed in the divine message of Moses said:

Our Lord! Pour out on us
Patience and constancy, and take our souls
Unto Thee as Muslims (who bow to Thy Will)!
(The Heights, 7: 126)

Of Jesus Christ and the disciples the Qur'an says:

When Jesus found unbelief on their part
He said: "Who will be my helpers
To (the work of) Allah?"
Said the Disciples:
"We are Allah's helpers:
We believe in Allah,
And do thou bear witness
That we are Muslims."
(The Family of 'Imran, 3: 52)

The Qur'an says that both Christ and his disciples are Muslims; Moses, the Egyptian magicians who were guided to believe in God, and Pharaoh, who repented on the point of death, are Muslims; Joseph, Abraham, Isma'il and Noah are all Muslims. The Arabic word for our religion, *Islam*, comes from the verb *aslama*, which means to surrender to the will of God, to submit to His power. But the noun *Islam* (literally *submission to God*) also implies the recognition that nothing truly exists except God, that He is the Absolute Monarch of all Being. The fact that the Qur'an uses the same word in referring to each and all is significant. It is deliberate and definitely meant to establish the identity of all religions. No distinction may therefore be made between one religion and another. The Qur'an goes even further to command that no distinction be made between one of God's messengers and another; no prophet should be more favored than any other.

The Messenger believeth
In what hath been revealed
To him from his Lord,
As do the men of faith
Each one (of them) believeth
In Allah, His angels,
His Books, and His Messengers.
"We make no distinction" (they say)
"Between one and another"
(The Heifer, 2: 285)

It would be fatuous to make distinctions between one apostle and another, for a good Christian is a Muslim, that is, he submits to God's will and recognizes His power, provided of course, that he believes in all prophets, Holy Scriptures, the Hereafter and that God is ONE. As has been said, all true religions are one as far as their essential creed is concerned. Their differences pertain only to the various stages of man's development that required progressively changing laws.

As for those who divide
Their religion and break up
Into sects, thou hast
No part in them in the least:
Their affair is with Allah.
(The Cattle, 6: 159)

Those who deny Allah and His Messengers,
And (those who) wish to separate Allah
From His Messengers, saying: "We believe in some
But reject others": And (those who) wish
To take a course midway –
They are in truth (equally) unbelievers
(The Women, 4: 150-151)

Because faith is indivisible, you cannot hope to be a true Muslim if you believe in one Book revealed by God but reject another. To be a Muslim is to accept all that God has sent down to all His prophets and all His books. Only thus could you be truly a believer in One God, and in all that He says (rather than in a critic of what He says).

Muslim mystics use beautiful expressions in referring to this religious unity. One may describe another as having a Christian, a Mosaic, or a Muhammadan "foot." Mystics say this about one another, though they all are Muslims. They thus show a deeper understanding of religious differences which are regarded not only as necessitated by the historical stages of man's development but also as expressions of the differences in the spiritual constitution which may exist among the members of a single community.

It is with such broadmindedness and breadth of outlook that religious multiplicity should be approached. Only thus, indeed, could we defeat fanaticism and recognize the ONE religion whose source is the One merciful God. God extends His mercy to any person who tries to reach Him. If a black man living in Africa had never heard of Muhammad or the Qur'an, if the only Scripture available was the Gospel translated into his native tongue and if he worshiped God according to the Gospel, God would understand his position and accept his worship. If an Eskimo had never heard of any revealed religion, but had tried hard and had recognized that God is One −perhaps by contemplating God's signs in the sky, believing the moon and stars to be symbolic of Divine Power, and perhaps hoping that by serving them to serve God − he will have his recompense in the other world. Any person who tries to reach God, by whatever means available to him, will be duly rewarded. God's Heaven is ready, with wide open doors, to receive all people who genuinely strive to reach Him. God tells us that He has sent down "warners" and "messengers" to every place on earth:

> *Thou art no other than a warner*
> *(The Creator, 35: 23)*

Some of these messengers may be identified as the prophets mentioned in the Qur'an, but the rest have never been specified. God tells Muhammad:

> *We did aforetime send Messengers before thee:*
> *Of them there are some whose story*
> *We have related to thee, and some whose story*
> *We have not related to thee.*
> *(Forgiver / The Believer, 40: 78)*

God has communicated His Word to everybody, everywhere, though in ways unknown to us. The relationship between God and His creation is an intimate one for us to understand fully. He sends down revelation not to man but also to animals.

> *And thy Lord taught the Bee*
> *To build its cells in hills,*
> *On trees, and in (men's) habitations*
> *(The Bee, 16: 68)*

Such are the close and intimate links between God and His creatures.

After the death of Prophet Muhammad (pbuh) many people claimed to be prophets. From time to time false prophets appeared, and some even claimed to have received a holy book. Most of these were duly hanged and their spurious books duly forgotten. The real challenge facing a fake prophet was to furnish evidence of his relationship with God, the Knower of the Unseen and the Visible. As the established legal practice puts the onus of proof on the claimant, the would-be messenger from the Knower of the Unseen must bring us fresh and genuine information from the Unseen. Evidently, if God sends down revelation to somebody, He must arm him with power over the people he is expected to guide, if not power over their natural laws. The latter would take the form of miracles or a holy book that would capture people's ears and hearts, and puzzle their minds. This was, of course, beyond the power of the fake messengers.

Now to surmount this insuperable problem, the pretenders to prophecy set out to destroy the very foundation of prophecy by denying the existence of the Unseen and the possibility of miracles. If they succeeded in doing that, the impostors thought there would be no way of putting their false claims to the test, so that they may join the Club of Prophecy unchallenged. But, as it was customary for every new prophet to recognize all foregoing prophets and their books, the new impostors had to recognize the Qur'an! To reconcile their recognition of the Qur'an with their denial of miracles and the Unseen, they had to come up with a heretical interpretation of the Qur'an to facilitate their misleading, destructive task.

They seem to have concurred on a so-called inward interpretation of the Qur'an. This means that they do not have to abide by the apparent meaning of the verses; indeed, they tend to discard the literal meaning of the verses altogether. So, according to this new-fangled interpretation, Devils in the Qur'an are symbolic of the physical senses, desires and passions; the angels are the good and benign thoughts; far from being real creatures, Satan is no more than a symbol of evil – the evil that dominates a man's soul; and the prophets' miracles reported in the Qur'an are allegorical, not factual occurrences. The stick of Moses was no more than the Mosaic Law, meant to lead and guide his people.

> He (Moses) said, "It is my rod:
> On it I lean; with it I beat down fodder
> For my flocks; and in it I find other uses.
> (Ta Ha, 20: 18)

The flocks are his people. The Qur'an says that when Moses cast down his stick, it turned into a snake that devoured all the magicians' false snakes. The impostors claim that this never happened in reality but that it is only an allegory. For here, they maintain, we have the power and proof of Divine Law devouring the snakes of falsehood. Did Moses not silence all opposition in this way?

When Moses struck the sea with his stick, the waters did not, according to them, part at all; the parting reported in the Qur'an must be interpreted as the parting of the ways, as the law of Moses (and his evidence, his staff) clearly parted right from wrong. When Moses, having drawn his hand close to His side, extended it white and shining without harm or stain, he was only in fact extending a symbolic, good hand to Pharaoh.

The resuscitation of the dead by Jesus is similarly interpreted as symbolic of the enlightenment of souls; he brought forth the ignorant into the light of knowledge rather than a dead man out of the grave. Restoring the sight of the blind man must be interpreted as equally allegorical, with blindness pertaining to the heart not to the eye. The table set with food that God sent down in answer to the prayer of Jesus is regarded as a symbol of intellectual food but no more.

In this way did Mirza Hussein Ali (who called himself Baha-ud-din) interpret the Qur'an to deprive it of the miraculous and the Unseen (the angels and the devils). As it has been mentioned, he did this to avoid being asked to perform a miracle or bring forth any information from the Unseen. He concluded that, far from performing miracles or having anything revealed from the Unseen, prophets were simply great social reformers who tried to help us live better. A prophet is a genius and his real miracle is social reform, obviously an open invitation to false prophets. Any reformer may thus claim to have received divine revelation.

It cannot be easily understood why Mirza calls this a "religion," in fact, the Baha'i Religion and insists that God "revealed" it to him. Surely it is no more than a social view, his own brain child, and no one can dispute his authorship. Why should he assert that he has intimations from the "Supernatural World" when he does not recognize the high beings of that world, including the angels? If he bases his argument on his failure to see the angels, the jinn, or the devils, he cannot claim that his case is the rule rather than the exception. Indeed, some chosen people have heard the jinn, seen the angels, spoken to the devils and witnessed the Unseen. Should a blind man's argument be binding on the sighted? Is it not true that the argument of a one-sighted person must be accepted by millions of blind people? If he can, and they cannot, see the sun, wouldn't the sun be there after all? Should we follow the opinion of the blind because they happen to be a majority? Should we appoint them to be judge of the highest pursuits of the human mind whose prime precondition is vision? How could a discipline be called a religion when it is established on the lack of vision, the preclusion of the miraculous, the non-existence of the angels and the devils?

The answer to these questions is this: they are all fabrications of a man who wanted to join the prophets' club without qualifications. He wanted to sneak his way into the Symposium of Immortals without passing the test. He denied the possibility of miracles and the Unseen to avoid presenting his credentials at the Divine Embassy he had invented.

This shows the grave danger inherent in the so-called inward interpretation of the Qur'an, of ignoring the literal sense and obvious meaning of the words. Such interpretation could result in uprooting religion properly conceived. It was resorted to by some sects in their internecine disputes, for example al-Khawarij (i.e., the Dissenters), al-Qaramitah (pertaining to Ibn Qarmut, the leader of a heretical sect with communist leanings), the Batiniyah (i.e., advocates of inward — Batini — interpretation) and the Babiyah. They manipulated the Qur'an to serve their own destructive purposes.

Now we must establish the right method of interpretation that should be followed meticulously: an interpreter must not deviate from the obvious meaning of the words, guided by the linguistic structure peculiar to Arabic. Any deviation from that sense to an inward or allegorical interpretation must be guided by other verses from the Qur'an. The Qur'an is interpreted in the light of the Qur'an, the hidden meaning coming to the surface with the help of the obvious meaning. Nowhere should our inward interpretation be in conflict with the obvious sense of the words. Indeed, the hidden meaning will never be acceptable unless it confirms and supports the obvious sense. No license is allowed unless absolutely necessary. Such is the method made imperative by the nature of this perfect Book where no word is allowed to precede, where it should succeed, another, unless absolutely necessary.

Only thus could we preserve the dignity of the Qur'an and the sanctity of the Prophecy. No one could pretend to be a new prophet when God has said that the Qur'an was revealed to the last of His Prophets.

Chapter 9

The Unseen

The Qur'an is unique in devoting long surahs (chapters) to information, reports, and facts that are simply enigmas, coming as they do from the world of the Unseen. They tax our rational faculties to the extreme; our minds can neither deny nor support them, and we are left with a difficult choice, to believe or not to believe because the facts presented lack all concrete evidence.

My own explanation is that they are designed, apart from being pieces of divine information revealed to us by God, to test the depth of our faith. To support this view, here is what the Qur'an has to say about the believers; they are:

> those who fear their Lord in their most secret thoughts
> (The Prophets, 21: 49)
>
> who believe in the Unseen
> (The Heifer, 2: 3)

These words, or words to the same effect, occur in many surahs. The true believers are those whose instrument of belief is their own hearts. They do not ask for material evidence, nor ask you to show them God so that they believe in Him, but believe in Him as Unseen, that is to say, in their hearts.

The Qur'an actually refers to man's inherent passion for argumentation as a far from commendable quality:

man is, in most things, contentious
(The Cave, 18: 54)

Religion is more of a feeling than a theory to be put to proof. It is essentially a state of mind rather than a rationalistic philosophy. To test this "state of mind" or this "attitude of heart," God presents us with a number of enigmas from the Unseen, things which can be neither proved nor disproved. Facing them we are plunged into paradox. We tend to reject and deny them, although we think that we are believers! The fact is that ours was no more than surface faith. It was based on a rational argument, pure and simple. Examples of these enigmas are: the Angels, the Jinn, the Hour, the Throne, the Chair, the Path, the Spirit, the Scales, the Tablet, the Pen, and the Barrier. Most enigmatic of all, of course, is the Devil himself, Satan and his tribe. God says:

> *He and his tribe watch you*
> *From a position where ye*
> *Cannot see them: We made the Evil Ones friends*
> *(Only) to those without Faith.*
> *(The Heights, 7: 27)*
>
> *If anyone withdraws himself*
> *From remembrance of (Allah) Most Gracious*
> *We appoint for him an evil one, to be*
> *An intimate companion to him.*
> *(The Gold Adornments, 43: 36)*

References to this satanic companion (or comrade) abound in the Qur'an. God tells us that on the Day of Resurrection, this devilish companion will appear to man. It is always a jinnee, and his function in this life is to tempt man to do evil. When the "companion" is shown to a person, regret would overcome that person who would say:

Would that between me and thee
Were the distance of East and West!
(The Gold Adornments, 43: 38)

This is indeed a very subtle verse. We know that the longest distance on earth is that between East and West. This verse says, however, the distance of the two Easts as an expression of the greatest measurable distance! It cannot, therefore, be properly interpreted unless it is assumed that the West, where the sun sets, is at the same time an East, where the sun rises somewhere else! And this could not be possible unless the earth was a globe that revolves around itself. If so, the distance of the two Easts must be the distance between the farthest two points on earth and even longer than that between the East and the West!

This is just an example of the Qur'an's subtlety. One needs to make a great effort to understand it. Such verses could never be properly interpreted at the time when they were revealed. It is also an indication that this business of the jinnee comrade, belonging as it does in the Unseen, could never be understood today. It must come to light at a later, preordained time. We must, however, believe it if we have healthy feelings, sensitive hearts, and spirits that remember a past existence in the Kingdom of Heaven. Indeed, to believe in the jinn and angel in your heart is to give evidence that you vaguely remember the Holy Kingdom of God. It is a faith which indicates a spiritual power, not a meaningless and inane acceptance.

God proceeds to tell us in the Qur'an that man is left alone with the evil jinnee comrade, but that he has another comrade, an angel, who inspires him with righteousness. This good angelic comrade, appears too on the Day of Resurrection to report on his human companion.

And his companion will say:
"Here is (his record) ready with me!"
(Qaf, 50: 23)

There are, besides these, recording angels, and watching angels who work in the service of man unseen:

But verily over you
(Are appointed angels) to protect you –
Kind and honorable –
Writing down (your deeds):
They know (and understand)
All that ye do.
(The Cleaving Asunder, 82: 10-12)

There are also the Angels of the Throne:

And the angels will be on its sides,
And eight will, that Day,
Bear the Throne
Of thy Lord above them.
(The Sure Reality, 69: 17)

How can eight angels carry the Throne of the Lord? Perhaps they are eight rows of numberless angels? Or could they be eight laws of physics or even metaphysics? Nobody knows. The Qur'an doesn't specify; it says "eight" pure and simple, without qualification.

Again, what is the Throne? Is it a symbol?

What is the Chair? God is described in the Qur'an thus:

His Throne doth extend
Over the heavens and the earth
(The Heifer, 2: 255)

This means that the Chair is vast enough to include the heavens and the earth with all their contents. If the Chair is so vast, how much vaster can be the Throne? How can creatures carry it above? Perhaps they are creatures of a kind completely unknown to us, perhaps they are huge electromagnetic beings? Aren't the sun and the stars held in position in cosmic space by the laws of gravity that appear, therefore, as huge hands and fingers? The Throne may be a figurative expression. Just as we say that the Ka'ba is the House of God, we may refer to something as God's Throne.

Then there is Gabriel, the angelic messenger and the Holy Spirit. It is reported that the Prophet saw him twice in his real form. It was a moonlit night when, walking alone in a place called al-Baqee', the Prophet saw the angel for the first time. At that moment, light drenched the horizon and filled up the sky above, whereupon, in awe, the Prophet fainted.

> For indeed he saw him
> At a second descent, near the Lote-Tree
> Beyond which none may pass
> (The Star, 53: 13-14)

As for Gabriel's qualities and power, the Qur'an says:

> Verily this is the word
> Of a most honorable Messenger
> Endued with Power,
> With rank before
> The Lord of the Throne.
> (The Folding Up, 81: 19-20)

The noble Messenger here is Gabriel who enjoys power and a secure position near the Lord of the Throne. He is also a teacher, and is again described as very powerful:

It is no less than
Inspiration sent down to him;
He was taught by one
Mighty in Power.
(The Star, 53: 4-5)

When God says that one of His creatures is very strong, that he is powerful and enjoys a secure power, that creature must be mighty indeed! From the Qur'an we understand that Gabriel may come down to the earth in any form and take revelation to any prophet, in any language, and at any age.

There are other angels, of course, of lesser rank, and each has a specific post or station. The Qur'an states:

(Those ranged in ranks say):
"Not one of us but has a place appointed."
(Those Ranged in Ranks, 37: 164)

That is to say, a single job or function. No angel has as many faculties and talents (and consequently varied functions) as man. Man is put higher in rank than many categories of angels. God "taught Adam the names, all of them" but when he asked the angels about them they said, "Glory be to Thee! We have no knowledge except what Thou Hast given us!" The names mentioned here are the variety of talents and branches of knowledge that secure man's superiority over other creatures.

God tells us that the angels have no sex. They are neither male nor female; they do not reproduce, nor eat or drink as we do. God stresses that they are neither His daughters nor sons but are His creatures. Indeed, how can He have children when He is the Lord of creation? He tells us, furthermore, that the angels are consistently obedient to God: they are deprived of man's freedom to disobey Him.

Who flinch not (from executing)
The Commands they receive from Allah,
But do (precisely) what they are commanded.
(Prohibition, 66: 6)

As for the jinn, God tells us that some of them are good and righteous, while others are evil disbelievers. There are male and female jinn who multiply. They can hear what goes on in the world of men and whisper to them. Some of them are rebels who try, driven by ambition, to listen to what goes on in the High Assembly of Heaven hoping to learn the Unseen but are hit by meteors and burned up. Some of them could do harm to man, but only if God wills it just as recovery from an illness must be at God's Will. It is blasphemous and ignorant, however, to try to placate the jinn, to curry favor with them or, indeed, to ask them to do favors (as help in recovery from illness) by offering sacrifices. To conjure up the jinn for worldly services will ultimately result in harm, not profit:

True, there were persons
Among mankind who took shelter
With persons among the Jinns,
But they increased them in folly.
(The Spirits, 72: 6)

This is how the jinn tell us in the Qur'an about their attempt at listening in:

And we pried into the secrets of heaven;
But we found it filled with stern guards and flaming fires.
We used, indeed, to sit there in (hidden) stations, to (seal)
A hearing, but any who listens now will find a flaming fire
Watching him in ambush.
And we understand not

Whether ill is intended to those on earth,
Or whether their Lord (really) intends
To guide them to right conduct.
There are among us some that are righteous,
And some the contrary:
We follow divergent paths.
(The Spirits, 72: 8-11)

The Qur'an stresses that the jinn are not acquainted with the Unseen, and that their attempts to listen consistently fail:

Indeed they have been removed
Far from even (a chance of)
Hearing it.
(The Poets, 26: 212)

And that they die, and will be resurrected and taken to look just like men. The Qur'an also tells us about the life of the jinn in the days of Solomon and how God put them in the service of His prophet:

And there were Jinns that worked in front of him,
By the leave of the Lord, and if any
Of them turned aside from Our Command,
We made him taste of the Penalty
Of the Blazing Fire.
They worked for him
As he desired (making Arches),
Images, Basins, as large as Reservoirs,
And (cooking) Cauldrons fixed (in their place):
"Work ye, sons of David, with thanks!
But few of my servants are grateful!"
(Sheba, 34: 12-13)

Regarding Solomon's taking of the Throne of the Queen of Sheba, the Qur'an says:

> Said one of the Jinns
> "I will bring it to thee
> Before thou rise from thy Council:
> Indeed I have full strength for the purpose,
> And may be trusted."
> Said one who had knowledge
> Of the Book: "I will bring it to thee
> Within the twinkling of any eye!"
> Then when (Solomon) saw it
> Placed firmly before him,
> He said: "This is by the grace of my Lord! –
> To test me whether I am
> Grateful or ungrateful!
> And if I am grateful,
> Truly his gratitude is (a gain)
> For his own soul; but if
> Any is ungrateful, truly
> My Lord is Free of All Needs,
> Supreme in Honor!"
> (The Ants, 27: 39-40)

We understand from the verse that he who has knowledge of the Book was more powerful than the jinn, because he transported the throne in a glance. We have another reference in the Qur'an to the ignorance of the jinn:

> Then, when We decreed (Solomon's) death,
> Nothing showed them his death except
> A little worm of the earth,
> Which kept (slowly) gnawing away
> At his staff: so when he fell down,

The Jinns saw plainly that
If they had known the unseen,
They would not have tarried
In the humiliating Penalty
(Of their Task).
(Sheba, 34: 14)

Here we have a man, Prophet Solomon, who dies standing, leaning on his staff, while the jinn all about him have no way of finding out whether he is dead or alive, and so continue to serve him unquestioningly. When a rodent or an insect comes and gnaws at the bottom of his stick, his body loses its balance and falls to the ground! Only then do the jinns realize that Solomon is dead. This is a proof of complete ignorance.

The Qur'an also tells us that God taught Solomon the languages of birds and ants:

At length, when they came
To a (lowly) valley of ants,
One of the ants said:
"O ye ants, get into
Your habitations, lest Solomon
And his hosts crush you
(Under foot) without knowing it."
So he smiled, amused at its speech;
And he said: "O my Lord! so order me
That I may be grateful for Thy favors,
Which Thou hast bestowed on me and on my parents,
And that I may work the righteousness
That will please Thee:
And admit me, by Thy Grace
To the ranks of Thy Righteous Servants."
(The Ants, 27: 18-19)

Such a reference to the language of ants was odd indeed in the past. We know better today. Science now tells us, on the basis of accurate observation and the actual biological evidence available, that ants and bees have distinct languages. In fact all insects that live in communities, cells, and organizations have some kind of language because without a common language it would be impossible for such innumerable hordes of insects to have an organized life and a perfect distribution of functions. It is quite possible for an ant to be conscious of Solomon's presence, just as Solomon knew of God's existence.

The Qur'an tells us that Satan was of the jinn, he and his tribe, but that they were given a lease of life until the Day of Resurrection: they would die in the end, then rise to live in Hell forever. It was the Devils who taught men to use magic, the magical tricks that could divide a man and his wife. The Qur'an explains that sorcery came first to the earth in old Babylon. Two angels, Harut and Marut, came down to the earth in human form to teach it. God wanted by revealing such mysteries to man, to tempt and try humankind. Indeed, the idea of trying the soul of man by temptation occurs quite frequently in the Qur'an:

> Every soul shall have a taste of death;
> And We test you by evil and by good
> By way of trial,
> To Us must ye return.
> (The Prophets, 21: 35)

It is to be noted that evil occurs in the verse before good, because it is more effective as a test. The story of Harut and Marut is told in the Qur'an:

They followed what the evil ones
Gave out (falsely)
Against the power
Of Solomon: the blasphemers
Were, not Solomon, but
The evil ones, teaching men
Magic, and such things
As came down at Babylon
To the angels Harut and Marut
But neither of these taught anyone
(Such things) without saying:
"We are only for trial;
So do not blaspheme."
They learned from them
The means to sow discord
Between man and wife.
But they could not thus
Harm anyone except
By Allah's permission.
And they learned what harmed them,
(The Heifer, 2: 102)

God stresses, therefore, that using black magic to hurt people cannot be effective unless God wills it. This includes an obvious, though implicit, admission of the existence of sorcery, apart from the facts relating to the time and place and method of its coming down to earth; but it condemns sorcery and sorcerers.

And the magician thrives not,
(No matter) where he goes.
(Ta Ha, 20: 69)

Is sorcery (like) this?
But sorcerers will not prosper.
(The Prophet Jonah [Yunus], 10: 77)

This sorcery about which the Qur'an speaks, which is again mentioned in the story of Moses and Pharaoh (when Pharaoh called the magicians to give the appearance of snakes to their staffs), and again in the story of the Samaritan (the Jew who used magic to make a golden calf that lowed), and again in referring to the evil women who blow on knots, is an old and extinct science. It differs completely from the babblings of magicians around us today. The old manuscripts where these mysteries were to be found have mostly perished. Similarly, very rare are those who can, and know properly how to, conjure up the jinn and put them in man's service. It is a knowledge that only brings suffering and destruction.

There are the phenomena of telepathy, clairvoyance, revelation, or epiphany. They are facts but are stranger than magic. Science records them without any rational explanation.

In the Qur'an, we hear of the *Barzakh* (literally *isthmus*) or partition, or barrier.

> *Before them is a Partition*
> *Till the Day they are raised up.*
> *(The Believers, 23: 100)*

This is the barrier that separates the spirits of the dead from the world of the living. The Qur'an throws light on it in two separate verses:

> *It is He Who has*
> *Let free the two bodies of flowing water:*
> *One palpable and sweet,*
> *And the other salty and bitter;*
> *Yet has He made a barrier between them,*
> *A partition that is forbidden to be passed.*
> *(The Criterion, 25: 53)*

The verse explains how rivers flow into the sea without getting salty: fresh water remains fresh in the river thanks to an isthmus (a barrier or a partition) between them. The same idea recurs elsewhere:

> *He has let free the two bodies*
> *Of flowing water, meeting together.*
> *Between them is a Barrier*
> *Which they do not transgress.*
> (*The Most Gracious, 55: 19-20*)

It is obvious that the Barzakh is not the actual isthmus, that is, the dividing stretch of land, as this does not prevent the rivers from flowing into the seas. The real Barzakh must refer to the law governing this process, namely that the sea level is much lower than that of the river because if the opposite were true, sea water would have flowed into the entire stretch of the river. Again, when sea water rises at one point in the tide cycle (under the influence of the gravitational pull of the moon), it flows into part of the river mouth. If the moon were nearer to the earth, a high tide would have caused sea water to flow into the length of the river, leaving us no fresh water to drink.

The Barzakh, the barrier or the ban, must refer to the physical laws that control, govern, and keep everything in place. This explains what the Qur'an has to say about the dead:

> *Before them is a Partition*
> *Till the Day they are raised up.*
> (*The Believers, 23: 100*)

The Barzakh should not, therefore, mean an actual physical barrier separating the spirits of the dead from the world of the living, but rather the laws that prevent any contact between the two worlds. The spirits start a new life after death and are governed by different laws, which makes it impossible for them and for us to communicate. Barzakh stands between us, and this must refer to the difference between our and their laws. The spirits may indeed be with us at a given point in time and place but communication will remain impossible because the laws of their existence differ from ours, there is a Barzakh between us.

Such verses as these throw light on the Qur'anic method of dealing with mysteries and the Unseen: it uses a code. Understandably, the Qur'an is not a book on hydraulics or physics and is not expected to go into scientific details. The Qur'an may use a single significant word, which would be sufficient, such as the word, *Barzakh*! It is beautiful because of its connotations and enhancing suggestiveness and it sets in motion a whole train of thought; it will be up to us in the end whether to believe or disbelieve.

Next come the Pen and the Tablet; God swears by the Pen and what is inscribed with it:

> *Nun, By the pen*
> *And by the (Record) which (men) write –*
> *(The Pen, 68: 1)*

This is not, however, the Pen which we, devil-inspired, use in writing articles. It is the Divine Pen that God uses in recording our destiny in the preserved Tablet, or it is the Pen used by the angels. According to the Qur'an, God writes and erases:

> *Allah doth blot out*
> *Or confirm what He pleaseth:*
> *With Him is The Mother of the Book.*
> *(The Thunder, 13: 39)*

It would indeed be puzzling if taken literally because these words appear to suggest that God is given to writing, blotting out, and changing His mind like the rest of us. This is far from true. The real interpretation must be that God is so merciful that He is prepared to overlook our sins to the extent of blotting them out if inspired by Him, we repent and mend our ways:

> *Those things that are good remove those that are evil.*
> *(The Prophet Hud, 11: 114)*

In this verse, the word *remove* can mean to *blot out*. Of course, God is free to do what He likes. He is in fact giving hope for all sinners to repent, coupling His absolute freedom with absolute mercy. We have further instances of such absolute freedom in what the Qur'an tells us about God's days. One verse says

> *A Day in the sight of thy Lord*
> *Is like a thousand years of your reckoning.*
> *(The Pilgrimage, 22: 47)*

but another,

> *The angels and the Spirit ascend*
> *Unto Him in a Day*
> *The measure whereof*
> *Is (as) fifty thousand years.*
> *(The Ways of Ascent, 70: 4)*

This means that the days of God are as long as God wants them to be. He may create a day that is one thousand years long, and another with the duration of fifty thousand years. He is not, as we are, governed by the times that He creates. He is above all time and absolutely transcendent. This is a lofty philosophical explanation of the meaning of eternity, of existing above, that is, outside, time.

These ideas flash like lightning in the few words used. One can easily miss them if one does not make the necessary effort, a tremendous effort equal to *Jihad* (dedicated struggle). Indeed, I believe that to read the Qur'an properly, one must engage in a kind of jihad. He who simply skims the Qur'an to reject it, only does injustice to himself and not to the Qur'an. The most profound ideas in the Qur'an are those concerned with the Unseen. A word, even a monosyllable, which you may pass by in a hurry, could reveal the entire secret of existence. There are deep meaningful facts at which you may scoff or reject offhand or relegate to the world of mythology and superstition simply because you regard yourself as an intellectual.

A saying by Christ provides an apt reply to this kind of attitude: "If thou dost according as thou knowest, God will reveal to thee what thou knowest not." In other words, if you act like a good student who reads all that is available and acts accordingly, you will be capable of understanding the words, which had appeared meaningless. It is the road taken by Muslim mystics who relied on revelations from God in unraveling some of the mysteries they encountered. But they knew that no revelation could come to them until they had read the Qur'an, acted accordingly, and called to God in humility. Mystics of the earlier era, had sought knowledge, worked for it, then waited for revelation. It is what the Qur'an promises:

> And those who strive in Our (Cause) –
> We will certainly guide them to Our Paths.
> (The Spider, 29: 69)

It is also what the Bible promises:

> Seek and thou shalt find;
> knock on the door and it will open.
> (Matthew, 7: 7)

Such knocking must be done whole-heartedly, not by murmuring a traditional prayer. As has been mentioned, God may be kind enough to you (as He is towards His favorite servants) to enable you to see the angels, witness the Unseen, and hear what no ear has ever heard.

> *If Allah had found in them any good,*
> *He would indeed have made them listen*
> *(The Spoils of War, 8: 23)*

> *So fear Allah; for it is Allah that teaches you.*
> *(The Heifer, 2: 282)*

God never breaks a promise, as we are wont to do:

> *We had already, beforehand,*
> *Taken the covenant of Adam,*
> *But he forgot; and We found*
> *On his part no firm resolve.*
> *(Ta Ha, 20: 115)*

Now we come to the most inscrutable article of the Unseen — the Hour, or Doomsday. When will the Hour come is the most difficult question of all. It has never been answered, and never will be. God has revealed its secret to no one, not even to His prophet.

> *They ask thee about the (final) Hour –*
> *When be its appointed time?*
> *Say: The knowledge thereof*
> *Is with my Lord (alone):*
> *(The Heights, 7: 187)*

It is knowledge that God keeps to Himself and has never imparted to any creature, and it is an awesome knowledge, as we shall see.

Chapter 10

The Hour

The Hour is the apex of the Unseen. No knowledge of it is revealed to anyone. Only God knows it. He tells us in the Qur'an, however, of certain conditions and signs of the Last Day. Some of these signs are thus specified:

Then watch thou for the Day
That the sky will bring forth
A kind of smoke (or mist)
Plainly visible.
Enveloping the people
This will be a Penalty Grievous.
(They will say:) "Our Lord!
Remove the Penalty from us,
For we do really believe!"
How shall the Message
Be (effectual) for them,
Seeing that a Messenger
Explaining things clearly
Has (already) come to them –
Yet they turn away from him
And say: "Tutored (by others),
A man possessed!"
We shall indeed remove
The Penalty for a while,
(But) truly ye will revert

(To your ways).
One day We shall seize
You with a mighty onslaught:
We will indeed (then)
Exact Retribution!
(The Smoke, 44: 10-16)

A reference to this smoke is made in the *Book of Revelation* which describes the opening of the abyss and the rising of smoke as though from a huge furnace, whereupon the sun and the atmosphere are darkened (Revelation 9: 2). We are further told that such smoke would not kill people but only torture them. People will seek death but cannot die. On this natural phenomenon both the Bible and the Qur'an concur.

The drift of this is a kind of smoke that will envelop the earth and clog sunlight; people will be in great pain for a limited period but God will relieve them. There are more signs in the Qur'an:

And when the Word is
Fulfilled against them (the unjust),
We shall produce from the earth
A Beast to (face) them; he will speak to them
(The Ant, 27: 82)

The Hour (of Judgement) is nigh;
And the moon is cleft asunder.
(The Moon, 54: 1)

God asks His Prophet to warn all evildoers against that Day:

Warn them of the Day
That is (ever) drawing near,
When the hearts will
(Come) right up to the throats

To choke (them);
No intimate friend nor intercessor
Will the wrongdoers have,
To whom can be listened.
(Forgiver / The Believer, 40: 18)

These signs will certainly remove any lingering doubts so that everybody must believe; the moon is split, and a beast has come out of the earth to speak! It will be too late for belief, however; it will be almost forced and will not count. People will have no option but to believe in anticipation of the rewards promised. How like opportunists who vie in declaring allegiance to a new regime once firmly established, in anticipation of material rewards! God will not accept this kind of loyalty:

The day that certain of the Signs
Of thy Lord do come,
No good will it do to a soul
To believe in them then,
If it believed not before
Nor earned righteousness
Through its Faith.
Say: "Wait ye; we too are waiting."
(The Cattle, 6: 158)

God always accepts the faith of those who believe in the Unseen, without question. The power of insight is above the power of sight, and the Unseen is the test of insight. Will the heart see what the eye cannot, and so believe and have faith in the Unseen? If a man does, he will prove his high rank, deep insight, and worthiness of salvation. If he doesn't, he will prove his inability to see, hear or think, except physically like an animal, thus determine his position at the bottom rung of the ladder.

The last sign is that of Gog and Magog. This is an enigmatic story, mostly allegorical, where the Qur'an tells of an errant conqueror Dhul Qarnayn (literally, *the man with the two horns or centuries*; *Qarn* in Arabic means either a *horn*, cf. Fr. Corne, or a *century*) who journeys on earth and arrives at a mysterious place somewhere between two barriers:

Until, when he reached
(A tract) between two mountains
He found beneath them, a people
Who scarcely understood a word.
They said: "O Dhu al Qarnayn!
The Gog and Magog (people)
Do great mischief on earth:
Shall we then render thee
Tribute in order that
Thou mightest erect a barrier
Between us and them?"
He said: "(The power) in which
My Lord has established me
Is better (than tribute):
Help me therefore with strength
(And Labor): I will erect a stronger
Barrier between you and them;
"Bring me blocks of iron."
At length, when he had
Filled up the space between
The two steep mountainsides,
He said, "Blow (with your bellows)."
Then when he had made
It (red) as fire, he said:
"Bring me, that I may
Pour over it, molten lead."

Thus were they made
Powerless to scale it or dig through it.
He said: "This is a mercy from my Lord:
But when the promise of
My Lord comes to pass,
He will make it into dust;
And the promise of my Lord is true."
On that day We shall
Leave them to surge
Like waves on one another;
The trumpet will be blown,
And We shall collect them
All together.
(The Cave, 18: 93-99)

It is a very mysterious story, and scholars commentators present us with two contradictory interpretations. Some say that Gog and Magog are the descendants of Yafith, son of Noah, and are actually the   yellow races that live in China and the neighboring lands. They had lived in ignorance and backwardness for centuries, while advanced peoples around them built up walls of science and industry. The melting of iron and lead by Dhul-Qarnayn must be a symbol of this. This means that they had lived, until the introduction of science, behind a wall, or a barrier, of backwardness. We are told that when the appointed time comes, they will put an end to that, establish iron and steel industries, build a hydrogen bomb, multiply into thousands of millions, destroy their wall (the barrier between them and the rest of the world) and conquer the earth in a war that must spell the end of life on this planet!

In the Bible are references to Gog and Magog, first in Ezekiel 38:2, then this in Revelation:

> *After the thousand years are over, Satan*
> *will be let loose from his prison, and he*
> *will go out to deceive the nations scattered*
> *over the whole world, that is, Gog*
> *and Magog. Satan will bring them altogether*
> *for battle, as many as the grains*
> *of sand on the seashore.*
> *(Revelation, 20: 7-8)*

What is that nation which, with a population like the grains of sand on the seashore, will be mustered to fight the world when the thousand years are over? In the Qur'an, we are told:

> *No one knows its true meanings except Allah.*
> *(The Family of 'Imran, 3: 7)*

God alone has the key to the code, as it were. He alone has knowledge of the Hour.

The Qur'an tells us that the Hour will come when earthly civilization has reached its apex and man has reached the apex of his progress. The earth will take on its glitter and deck itself fair; man will think that he has control of, and the power to do, anything! He will be able to control rainfall, cultivate the desert, treat incurable diseases, transplant hearts and eyes, travel between planets, split the atom and move mountains. God warns us:

> *(It grows) till the earth –*
> *Is clad with its golden ornaments*
> *And is decked out (in beauty):*
> *The people to whom it belongs*
> *Think they have all powers*
> *Of disposal over it:*
> *There reaches it Our command*

By night or by day,
And We make it
Like a harvest clean-mown,
As if it had not flourished
Only the day before!
Thus do We explain
The Signs in detail
For those who reflect.
(The Prophet Jonah [Yunus], 10: 24)

The verse is subtle. God says that the Hour will come by night or day, which can only be explained if we assume that the earth is a revolving globe, half of it experiencing daylight and the other night. When the Hour comes, it will be a twinkling.

And the Decision of the Hour (of Judgement)
Is as the twinkling of an eye, or even quicker.
(The Bees, 16: 77)

Half the population of the earth will have day and the other half night. The statement would not have been precise if it said that the Hour would come simply by day, or alternatively by night. To ensure the semantic precision of a promise which must be honored, God uses the subtle expression, "by night or by day." And to underline the importance of this subtle reference, the Qur'an says elsewhere:

Say: "Do ye see –
If His punishment should come
To you by night or by day,
What portion of it
Would the sinners
Wish to hasten?"
(The Prophet Jonah [Yunus], 10: 50)

The sudden chastisement that God says again, will come by night or day is an invitation for us to think for ourselves.

Now the Qur'an gives the last sign of the Hour, namely the blowing of the Trumpet and the Resurrection. The scenes of Doomsday as rendered in the Qur'an are spine chilling. The sun and moon are eclipsed, mountains are blown up, stars are darkened, the seas explode, the earth quakes, and all living beings in the heavens and the earth are struck by lightning, with the exception of those who will be saved by God to witness the horrors of that day.

All this will happen with the first blow of the Trumpet, the second blow will revive all the dead for the reckoning to begin.

In the Bible, there is a similar picture of Doomsday:

> And I saw the Lamb break open the sixth seal.
> There was a violent earthquake,
> and the sun became black like coarse
> black cloth, and the moon turned
> completely red like blood. The stars fell
> down to the earth, like unripe figs
> falling from the tree when a strong wind
> shakes it. The sky disappeared like
> a scroll being rolled up, and every
> mountain and island was moved from its place.
> (Revelation, 6: 12-14)

In the Qur'an, Doomsday is thus described:

> When the Sky is rent asunder,
> And hearkens to (the Command of) its Lord –
> And it must needs (do so) –
> And when the Earth is flattened out,
> And casts forth what is within it
> And becomes (clean) empty
> (The Rending Asunder, 84: 1-4)

When the sun
(With its spacious light)
Is folded up,
When the stars fall, losing their lustre
When the mountains vanish
(Like a mirage);
When the she-camels,
Ten months with young
Are left untended;
When the wild beasts
Are herded together
(In human habitations);
When the oceans
Boil over with a swell
(The Folding Up, 81: 1-6)

In all verses about Doomsday, the Qur'an tells us that God and the angels come down. Indeed, Doomsday always appears to me as a bigger version (that is, on a larger scale and with colossal dimensions) of the incident wherein Moses asked to see his Lord. The Qur'an tells us what happened then:

He said: "O my Lord!
Show (Thyself) to me,
That I may look upon Thee.
Allah said: "By no means
Canst thou see Me (directly);
But look upon the mount;
If it abide in its place,
Then shalt thou see Me.
When his Lord manifested
His glory on the Mount,
He made it as dust,
And Moses fell down in a swoon.
(The Heights, 7: 143)

The same things appear to be magnified in all images of Doomsday:

> They ask thee concerning the Mountains:
> Say, "My Lord will uproot them
> And scatter them as dust;
> He will leave them as plain
> Smooth and level.
> (Ta Ha, 20: 105-106)

> Will they wait
> Until Allah comes to them
> In canopies of clouds,
> With angels (in His train)
> And the question
> Is (thus) settled?
> (The Heifer, 2: 210)

> And the sky will be
> Rent asunder, for it will
> That Day be flimsy.
> And the angels will be
> On its sides,
> And eight will, that Day,
> Bear the Throne
> Of thy Lord above them.
> (The Sure Reality, 69: 16-17)

> Nay! When the earth
> Is pounded to powder,
> And thy Lord cometh
> And His angels
> Rank upon rank
> (The Dawn, 89: 21-22)

And the heavens shall be opened
As if there were doors,
And the mountains shall vanish,
As if they were a mirage.
(The Great News, 78: 19-20)

The Trumpet will (just)
Be sounded, when all
That are in the heavens
And on earth will swoon,
Except such as it will
Please Allah (to exempt).
Then will a second one
Be sounded, when, behold,
They will be standing
And looking on!
And the Earth will shine
With the glory of its Lord:
The Record (of Deeds)
Will be placed (open);
The prophets and the witnesses
Will be brought forward;
And a just decision
Pronounced between them;
And they will not
Be wronged (in the least)
(Crowds, 39: 68-69)

There will be a Divine Presence, such as had struck Moses down and destroyed the mountain. This time, however, everybody will be struck down and all the mountains will evaporate. Elsewhere God speaks of stones:

which sink for fear of Allah.
(The Heifer, 2: 74)

It appears that Doomsday is nothing but the revelation of God's face whereupon all forms of matter, unable to bear such power, will melt away. Nothing can stand firm in God's presence. The mountains will wilt away in humility, first bending down then evaporating altogether as if a mirage. All forms of life will be struck down; there won't be a single voice or the slightest sound of life as God lifts the veil and reveals His glory. We come across this in the Bible:

> The city has no need of the sun or the
> moon to shine on it, because the glory
> of God shines on it, and the Lamb is like a lamp.
> (Revelation, 21: 23)

It is the "glory" which the creatures could not withstand in the beginning and so were struck down, and were then resuscitated by God in another life for the reckoning.

> From changing your Forms
> And creating you (again)
> In (Forms) that ye know not.
> (The Inevitable, 56: 61)

This means that this second rising will be different and take a shape unknown to us. The Qur'an always speaks about a meeting between each man and his Lord:

> And every one of them
> Will come to Him singly
> On the Day of Judgement.
> (Mary, 19: 95)

> And behold! ye come to Us bare and alone
> As We created you for the first time
> (The Cattle, 6: 94)

O thou man!
Verily thou art ever
Toiling on towards thy Lord–
Painfully toiling–but thou
Shalt meet Him.
(The Rending Asunder, 84: 6)

As for those who sell
The faith they owe to Allah
And their own plighted word
For a small price,
They shall have no portion
In the Hereafter; nor will Allah
(Design to) speak to them
Or look at them
On the Day of Judgement,
Nor will He cleanse them
(Of sin); they shall have
A grievous Penalty.
(The Family of 'Imran, 3: 77)

And leave Me (alone to deal with)
(The Enfolded One, 73: 11)

And fear Allah,
And know that ye are
To meet Him (in the Hereafter)
And give (these) good tidings
To those who believe.
(The Heifer, 2: 223)

Whoever expects to meet his Lord,
Let him work righteousness, and,
In the worship of his Lord,
Admit no one as partner.
(The Cave, 18: 110)

Such an encounter could not take place if we still kept our human forms. If it did, it would be a Doomsday on which all creatures will be struck down, the mountains and seas destroyed, and *"the Earth will be changed to a different Earth, and so will be the Heavens" (The Prophet Abraham, 14: 48)*. As the Biblical book of Revelation states:

> *Then I saw a new heaven and a new*
> *earth. The first heaven and the first*
> *earth disappeared, and the sea vanished.*
> *(Revelation, 21: 1)*

Concerning the significance of the Arabic word for *Resurrection, Qiyamah,* literally meaning *rising* is directly related to that beautiful name of God *Qayyoum* which means *eternal* in the sense that He is always present. To be in His presence, therefore, having risen to Him, is the literal meaning of *Resurrection.* And to be in his presence is to be conscious of nothing else except that presence.

> *Whose will be the Dominion that Day?*
> *That of Allah, the One, the Irresistible!*
> *(Forgiver / The Believer, 40: 16)*

The illusory kingdom, in which each of us had lived, as his own, on earth, will have come to an end. Each of us had acted as a king, even as a god, with a kingdom and subjects to rule over; each had heady ideas about himself and the thought that he was all in all. But now the kingdom is in the hands of the real King, the Creator who had made everything and to whom everything must return. The key word in all this is God's presence. Indeed, Doomsday can mean nothing more than that God will reveal Himself, will appear truly. It is true that God is always present, everywhere, but there is a difference between omnipresence and the revelation of Him.

With this revelation everything will be completely crushed and all material forms will perish. No form of matter can possibly survive the immediate presence of God in His Oneness and Perfection.

We have heard of various new interpretations in the light of scientific theories of Doomsday: the moon hitting the earth; the sun dying out; the shrinking, burning up or expansion of the universe in space; or matter crashing into anti-matter. It is all, I believe, unnecessary. Man does die in the end, with or without reason. And just as death comes to the individual, it comes to a nation, to a civilization, to whole breeds of animals, and to the stars in their orbits. We need not trouble our minds with the reason for the end. It comes in accordance with a law decreed by the Maker who made everything. When the Maker tells us that there will be a Doomsday, we shouldn't bother with the reasons. Above all, we should not seek justifications because it is the one and only absolute Commander who will have it done.

The Trumpet Blast is only a symbol of the Command. We have many names for it in the Qur'an: it is now represented by a blow in a Trumpet (we hear of the Trumpet Sounded), now by a Scare, an Earth Tremor, or a Clatter. They all stand for a simple Command: *"Be, and it is."*

The Command has arrived; that is all. It is the law. Everything is doomed. Each one of us has a minor Doom, Death. But there is a major Doom, when time will melt away into Eternity, and everything is returned to the source. There cannot be a shadow of doubt. There is every possible reason and ample proof for each person to believe in his or her own heart, without arguing, without questioning.

Chapter 11

Resurrection

Addressing His Prophet in the Qur'an, God says:

Truly thou wilt die (one day),
And truly they (too) will die (one day).
(Crowds, 39: 30)

The meaning is obvious because *dead* means *wilt, mortal*, etc., (and most translations have paraphrased it). But the actual word in Arabic (not withstanding the obvious, or surface meaning) is *dead*, and its implication is all-important. It can thus be interpreted: "You live through God, you hear and speak through God, just like all mortal men. Everyone lives through God, sees through God, and hears through God, but is in himself dead because he has no independent life in himself. Each and all depend for existence on the one God who is the Creator and who, All-Sufficient, needs nothing."

The statement "Thou art dead" is violent enough to awaken the sense: it brings you face to face with a terrible reality – a present not a future state. Each one of us is carrying this corpse on his shoulders (i.e., to the grave). In every drop of perspiration and saliva, he casts away a dead piece of his body, just as a tree sheds its dead leaves everyday. Death is at every moment present, at every moment adjourned. The only living reality is God. We live literally on borrowed time, on a loan of life that, advanced by God, must be repaid sometime. God thus addresses Muhammad in a Qudsi hadith:

> Live as thou wilt; thou wilt die,
> love whomsoever thou wilt: thou wilt leave them;
> possess whatever thou wilt: it is buried in the dust;
> work as thou wilt: your work will be thy companion.

Love leads to heartache because we inevitably leave our loved ones. Unless love for God encompasses all other love, love is in vain. Material wealth is in vain because we shall inevitably depart from our possessions. The only thing that accompanies us is our work. The warning of death, of mortality, is repeated dozens of times in the Qur'an to draw our attention to the obvious and certain fact of life's end. Ours is a finite life, although nobody seems to heed to it. We all live and act as though we're immortals and this is the cause of avarice, mendacity, robbery, murder, tyranny, and despotism. The offenders believe they are secure and will live forever.

The Qur'an states that the majority are wrong and ignorant. In matters of faith, it warns us not to pursue the path of the majority because most people may know how to eat and drink but not how to reach the truth:

> But most of them follow nothing but fancy:
> Truly fancy can be of no avail.
> (The Prophet Jonah [Yunus], 10: 36)

> Yet the greater part of men refuse (to receive it)
> Except with ingratitude.
> (The Night Journey, 17: 89)

Most of them We found not
Men (true) to their covenant
But most of them We found
Rebellious and disobedient.
(The Heights, 7: 102)

Wert thou to follow the common run
Of those on earth, they will lead
Thee away from the Way of Allah.
They follow nothing but conjecture:
They do nothing but lie.
(The Cattle, 6: 116)

Or thinkest thou that most
of them listen or understand?
They are only like cattle –
Nay, they are worse astray in Path.
(The Criterion, 25: 44)

The word is proved true
Against the greater part of them;
For they do not believe
(Yaseen, 36: 7)

He has brought them the Truth,
But most of them hate the Truth.
(The Believers, 23: 70)

If Muhammad had started the call to Islam by inviting the people of Makkah to a referendum on the single question of "God or your idols?," the overwhelming majority would have chosen idols. The recognition of the truth will always be the prerogative of the elite. You can, however, refer to the majority in all questions pertaining to the business of living, food and drink, money and reproduction. They know these things well and instinctively vie to attain greater portions of them. But wasn't it the majority that voted in the past for the execution of Socrates, the burning of St. Bruno, and the imprisonment of Galileo, when given a chance to pronounce on matters of philosophy, faith, and science? With their usual mob mentality, most people cannot comprehend why a scientist may spend his whole life studying a worm or dissecting an ant. A mob mentality finds it difficult to see that such studies may lead to a series of researches culminating in the discovery of a special vaccine to combat cancer, cystic fibrosis, or influenza.

Most people seek immediate and concrete profit; they are the slaves of their wants and desires. Consider the example of a scientist who seeks the opinion of the majority in electromagnetic problems. It will be unfair to the majority, to him, and to electromagnetism. Leadership in matters of thought and science belongs rightly to the elite. Any course of action must be decided, however, by consultation among all scientists and intellectuals, not dictated by a single individual:

> And consult them in affairs (of moment).
> (The Family of 'Imran, 3: 159)

> Who (conduct) their affairs by mutual consultation
> (Consultation, 42: 38)

> Thou art not one to overawe them by force.
> (Qaf, 50: 45)

> Then he looked round;
> Then he frowned and he scowled
> (The One Wrapped Up, 74: 21-22)

> We worship none but Allah,
> That we associate no partners with Him.
> (The Family of 'Imran, 3: 64)

The Qur'an is against what is today described as the "individual cult," and against dictatorship, even if the individual happens to be a prophet. The rule is consultation, cooperation, and brotherhood.

The Believers are but a single Brotherhood.
(The Chambers, 49: 10)

Help ye one another in righteousness and piety
But help ye not one another in sin and rancor
(The Repast, 5: 2)

Allah doth command you
To render back your Trusts
To those to whom they are due;
And when ye judge between man and man,
That ye judge with justice
(The Women, 4: 58)

The Qur'an emphasizes that there are different classes of people. But these are not defined in terms of material possessions (capital, real estate, or income), but in terms of their varying shares of knowledge, education and piety. Spirits are never equal, even if the bodies have equal claims to the human rights of justice, sufficiency, etc.

Allah will raise up,
To (suitable) ranks (and degrees),
Those of you who believe
And who have been
Granted knowledge.
(The Plea of a Woman, 58: 11)

Those Messengers
We endowed with gifts,
Some above others
(The Heifer, 2: 253)

The most honored of you in the sight of Allah
Is (he who is) the most righteous of you.
(The Chambers, 49: 13)

For all these swift indicators, the Qur'an has not laid down a definite political system, but allowed people to resort to interpretation, because temporal political systems are changeable. Indeed, all systems are designed to suit specific times and they change all the time! The Qur'an is, however, a timeless book including timeless knowledge and lasting facts but caring little for temporal matters. The Qur'an is a book on religion and ethics rather than politics. Even so, it does offer general guidelines which ensure good government:

Individual freedom must be sanctified. The elite
Should be in charge of all matters pertaining to the
Intellectual and cultural life of the nation;
The majority be consulted in matters directly
Related to the business of living. Government by the
Elite should be based on consultation not tyranny; it
Should aim at securing justice and economic sufficiency,
At combating iniquity and exploitation.

The method to be adopted in applying these principles and the political details entailed are open to discussion. Interpretation is invited. The Qur'an makes no reference to such details. After all, the Qur'an is a book addressed to the heart of the individual. It seeks to guide and save the individual so that the group of individuals we call society may be guided and saved ultimately. In other words, it does not seek to improve the individual but takes its point of departure in individual hearts and minds. Rather than knock on the door of politics to change a society, the Qur'an knocks on the door of the heart to guide the individual. Of the individual, the Qur'an says:

> If anyone slew a person –
> unless it be for murder
> Or for spreading mischief in the land –
> It would be as if he slew the whole people.
> And if anyone saved a life, it would be
> As if he saved the life of the whole people.
> (The Repast, 5: 32)

To kill a single individual unjustly and wrongfully, even though for the purpose of ensuring material gains or reforms, is to destroy a divine law and slay all of mankind. Such is the value of the individual in Qur'anic law. The individual is an absolute entity in himself who has dignity, sanctity, and freedom. Respect for this freedom is the prime prerequisite of real worship.

It is true that a person dies physically in this world, but spiritually he has absolute life on another plane. He has immortality. He cannot be regarded merely as a cog in the social wheel or a screw that may be removed and replaced at will, whatever the modern slogans may be used to justify this. Slogans change with worldly systems, but the spirit of man is immortal. It should be respected in itself and for itself.

It is this admirable sanctification of the individual and of individual freedom that distinguishes all religion from the materialist creed of Marxism that preaches that an individual has no real existence and is doomed to nothingness, being merely the outcome of his age, circumstances and society. The Marxist materialists believe that the human soul consists of a group of reactions, of circumstantial and conditional reflexes; that it serves the body and is completely dependent upon it, that the sensation of hunger is designed to provide the body with food; and that sexual stimulation is meant to ensure physical reproduction. When the body dies, they assert, the soul dies with it. The Spirit they regard as a meaningless, mystical superstition. According to the Marxist, materialistic philosophy, there is no such a thing as a spiritual, immortal life beyond the mortal life of this world. This life is all there is, with nothing before or after: we consist of nothing apart from our bodies. Consequently, individuals may be regarded as nuts and bolts in the social machine and, if they do not serve their purpose, they may be sacrificed. Society is believed to be the immortal reality, the individual as a dispensable entity whose value rests in what it does for society.

I believe that this view requires careful examination. Is it true that we consist of nothing beyond our bodies and that the whole world is pure matter?

The materialists argue that in the beginning matter developed into man and that tomorrow this man will die and the play will have had its final curtain! As simple as that! These are objective facts, they argue. The body, however, is a very objective thing that may be studied, examined, and dissected. Unfortunately for the Marxists, they resort to oversimplification even if facts are distorted in the process. They wouldn't do so much as look under their own skin to see what is inside their selves. That the body is not the whole man and that inside it a soul exists is not an objective fact but is, by definition, subjective. The Marxist may ask, "What is that subjective entity which you call a self or a soul? It is, isn't it, the sum total of physical desires: hunger, fear, sex, and the sensory mechanisms of the body which, being physical appendages, must be regarded as equally objective?"

The question is: objective to whom? Are we to believe that these appendages are objective because other people perceive them? But are they perceived at all? Other people in fact assume their existence by interpreting behaviorist phenomena, which can be misleading. Don't we dissemble? Don't we continually resort to play-acting to the extent that our outward behavior rarely ever reflects our real thoughts and feelings?

No, the criterion of other people is not watertight!

Well, perhaps these appendages are objective as viewed by the individual himself? They are, in other words, an object as viewed by the subject.

But how can you treat yourself as an object? If you do, the self will grow cold. Under the sharp strokes of analytic lancets, the self will turn into a corpse and the soul will run away. The soul cannot be removed from microscopic scrutiny like a tree leaf. Its essence is its subjectivity and its reality consists in its being the other side of the coin. It is the subject because the body is the object. Subject and object being the two poles of reality, to define matter as objective is to admit the existence of something other than matter, namely the soul.

In the light of this fact, we cannot accept the materialistic definition of self and soul. They cannot be reduced to mere physical drives, the hunger, sex, and fear with which the body recognizes thirst and hunger, etc. Nothing can be farther from the truth of man and his soul.

Man does sacrifice his livelihood, his home, and his warm bed for targets and ideals that are abstract in the extreme as justice, right, and freedom! Are we to equate the ideals of justice and freedom with hunger and sex? Are we to assume that workers sacrifice themselves because they are driven by those physical needs alone? Should we not assume, rather, that there is another entity that dictates such a course of action? Rather than the "physical needs reflected in an inner mirror," the soul is a transcendent reality. It exists beyond and above the body, and it is the colossal power which sacrifices the body but is never subservient to it!

If you were to be equated solely with your body, you'd be hard-pressed to explain how you control and subject that body. If you merely were your hunger, you would not be able to control that hunger. The simple fact that you have an inner power capable of controlling your physical life and your instincts means that you have, within you, a distinctly different element that we call the self.

— with your soul you control your body

— with your mind you control your soul

— with your insight you control your mind.

This differentiation between one mode of existence and another, between an existent and a super-existent that controls it, is the actual proof of the existence of the spirit as a transcendent reality, as a power independent of the body but which controls it. The spirit is not dependent on, nor does it die with, the body.

He who claims that a man is merely a combination of physiological (material) functions must explain to us where that man goes at the moment he sinks to sleep. All physiological functions continue during sleep, and so do all the reflexes. If you prick the hand of the sleeping man with a pin, the hand will immediately react away from you; the heart continues to beat; breathing is regular; gland secretions do not cease; the movement of the bowels goes on; and the genitals respond to stimulation. Yet what we have now is a sleeping man who may be compared to a tree or an animal; he has primitive life that is as close as could be to insect life. Where is the real man?

The cycle of sleep and wakefulness is a miniature of life's bigger cycle of death and resurrection. It reveals the existence of that transcendent element which, once back in wakefulness, could restore to the outstretched body, suddenly and without preliminaries: a Hitler, a Nero, or a Caligula. Such an apparently lifeless body now wakes up to kill, invade and destroy! We cannot, can we, explain the astounding difference between the two conditions in terms of materialistic changes occurring in a split second?

The Qur'an plausibly explains what happens. The Qur'an tells us that the spirit leaves the body in sleep, just as happens in death, and then comes back in wakefulness:

It is Allah that takes
The souls (of men) at death;
And those that die not
(He takes) during their sleep:
Those on whom
He has passed the decree
Of death, He keeps back
(From returning to life),
But the rest He sends
(To their bodies)
For a term appointed.
Verily in this are Signs
For those who reflect.
(Crowds 39: 42)

The Qur'an is full of verses that decisively establish the reality of Resurrection, of life after death:

And Allah has produced from the earth,
Growing (gradually), and in the End
He will return you into the (earth)
(The Prophet Noah, 71: 17-18)

Verily We shall give life to the dead,
And We record that which they sent before
And that which they leave behind,
And of all things have We taken account
In a clear Book (of Evidence).
(Yaseen, 36: 12)

The trumpet shall be sounded,
When behold! from the sepulchres (men)
Will rush forth to their Lord!
They will say: "Ah! woe unto us!
Who hath raised us up
From our beds of repose?...
(A voice will say:)
"This is what (Allah)
Most Gracious had promised,
And true was the word of the messengers!"
It will be no more than a single Blast, when lo!
They will all be brought up before Us!
(Yaseen, 36: 51-53)

"Did ye then think
That We had created you in jest,
And that ye would not be
Brought back to Us (for account)?"
(The Believers, 23: 115)

They will come forth –
Their eyes humbled –
From (their) graves, (torpid)
Like locusts scattered abroad.
(The Moon, 54: 7)

One Day We shall remove the mountains,
And thou wilt see the earth as a level stretch,
And We shall gather them, all together,
Nor shall We leave out any one of them.
And they will be marshalled
Before their Lord in ranks, (with the announcements),
"Now have ye come to Us (bare) as We created you
First: aye, ye thought We shall not fulfill
The appointment made to you to meet (Us)!"
(The Cave, 18: 47-48)

So, by thy Lord,
Without doubt, We shall
Gather them together, and also
The Evil Ones (with them);
Then shall We bring them
Forth on their knees
Round about Hell
(Mary, 19 :68)

To recapitulate: The spirit is a fact. It is transcendent to the body and secure from mortality. Immortal, it will go back to its Creator on the Day of Resurrection. It was oversimplification on the part of the Marxists that produced their false image of man. In an attempt to find an easy solution to an insuperable problem they have distorted all facts, claiming that man is no more than his body, that he is made of dust and must go back to dust. Is anything done in vain? Does anything at all perish forever and go to utter waste? How can anyone believe that man, the noblest of all God's creatures, will perish forever and go to utter waste?

"Did ye then think
That We had created you in jest,

And that ye would not be
Brought back to Us (for account)?"
(The Believers, 23: 115)

Does man think that he will be left uncontrolled
(without purpose)?
(The Resurrection, 75: 36)

A disbeliever came to Prophet Muhammad with a dead man's bone, crushed it into powder, and asked, "Will your God resuscitate these bones now that they are dust?"

A Revelation came down to Muhammad, some time later, with the following verse:

And he makes comparisons for Us,
And forgets his own (Origin and) Creation;
He says, "Who can give life to (dry) bones
And decomposed ones (at that)?"
(Yaseen, 36: 78)

The Qur'an here adduces irrefutable proof. One may ask how God creates a new life out of decayed bones but, he forgets that he himself was created from nothing but a drop of water! Surely He who has created you in the first place must be capable of bringing you back to life.

Is not He, who created the heavens and earth,
Able to create the like thereof? –
Yes indeed! For He is the Creator Supreme,
Of skill and knowledge (infinite)!
(Yaseen, 36: 81)

Were We then weary with the first Creation,
That they should be in confused doubt
About a new Creation?
(Qaf, 50: 15)

To paraphrase, God says that it was not difficult to create men originally, and it cannot be difficult to resurrect them. Men should never doubt God's ability to do that:

We produced the first Creation, so
Shall We produce a new one
(The Prophets, 21: 104)

The story of Resurrection is thus, clearly but briefly, told by the Qur'an. In what I may describe as an exciting verse, God tells us about the rising of the dead after their long sleep in their graves:

On the Day that the Hour (of reckoning)
Will be established,
The transgressors will swear
That they tarried not
(The Romans, 30: 55)

The centuries that the dead have spent in their graves will appear to them on Resurrection as no longer than minutes. They will feel as though they have had an afternoon nap or a siesta after a heavy lunch. To every person Resurrection will appear as taking place immediately after death, because on his death he steps out of time and space, being unconscious of the time spent in the grave. It is not, therefore, an exaggeration to state that for each of us Resurrection is just as far away as the time of death, and it is that, in this sense, very near indeed.

Perchance the Hour is nigh!
(The Confederates, 33: 63)

This concept may equally explain the verse of Resurrection:

And your creation or your resurrection
Is in no wise but as an individual soul
(Luqman, 31: 28)

The raising up of Alexander the Great from his grave, where he had been dead for two thousand years, and the raising up of the beggar who passed away only yesterday, are like the raising up of a single person: the time spent by both in the grave will be felt by neither. It is as though, therefore, they died on the same day and, now they are resurrected at the same moment.

Though established fact, the spirit and resurrection are problematic enough, and today's readers may require additional philosophical evidence of their existence. So, for the philosophically minded reader, let me adduce such proof. In dealing with the spirit, I am going to rely on the well-known qualities of movement.

As is well known, movement can only be observed externally. If you are moving at the same pace and within the same orbit as another moving object, you will fail to observe its movement. You must step outside the orbit and stand still before you can observe it. Sometimes, you must admit, you cannot tell whether the elevator that you are inside is moving or still; but, you can tell, if you look outside at a fixed platform or landing. The same thing applies to the moving train and the sun! You can see them moving in relation to Earth, if you first fly into space; you cannot observe a condition wherein you are involved.

The process of perception is a definite proof of the existence of two things at the same time: the object perceived, and the perceiving subject. Consequently, we would never have been able to perceive the passage of time unless there was a perceiving subject within us capable of stepping outside to observe its movement from a separate platform, something stationary outside the flux of time.

If our perception moved consistently with the hands of the clock as they ticked the seconds away, we would never be able to perceive those seconds. Our perception would have moved on with the seconds, elapsing with them, without observing anything. This is a stunning conclusion that must be pondered thoroughly.

Man's reality is twofold. The physical part is immersed in time and elapses with time, gets older and feebler everyday and dies in the end (the body). The spiritual part lives outside time, observing it from a stationary platform without ever getting involved in it; it never ages, weakens, or elapses. When the body falls prey to time and is reduced to dust, the spirit still remains outside time, that is, alive.

Every one of us can feel that living entity within himself. Every one can realize that it is different in kind from external entities that change continually. Every person can feel that he has inside him a condition of being – presence, duration, or permanence – which is completely different from the time-controlled material existence. The inner mental state, which I have called a "condition of presence," is the key to the spiritual being within. It unravels the mystery of the spirit, the absolute, the ultimate.

Our aesthetic and moral sense is a case in point. When we perceive beauty or an act of righteousness and justice, we actually distinguish it from ugliness or wrongdoing and iniquity, using a criterion that is independent of all these things. To have a sense of discrimination is to be able to take a position on our "spiritual platform."

The existence of the spirit can, therefore, be proved by the existence of the conscience, of the aesthetic sense, and that mysterious faculty with which we distinguish right from wrong, the false from the real, the moral sense.

Is this platform to remain outside time forever? Perhaps it belongs to a different time scale where a day can be as long as a thousand years? The Qur'an says,

> *"And surely a day with thy Lord*
> *Is as a thousand years of your reckoning."*
> *(Pilgrimage, 22: 47).*

Scholars have been in conflict over the exact meaning of God's days, which are impossible to understand. References to God's days are mostly symbolic and oblique indicators. Time and space are relevant only in our own dimension, not in the spiritual realm.

Can the spirit reside in the aesthetic sense planned in us by God as proof of His consummate workmanship? It may be a spark of His Spirit, forever alive in us since He breathed His Spirit into us. It may be a holy flame derived from His light, a ray from His eternal sun? In trying to fathom the depth of that mystery, man is made only too conscious of the sad incompetence of human speech.

We would not be far wrong if we defined the spirit within us as our freedom, an inner inveterate freedom living in the deeper recesses of the soul. The Creator wants it to be absolutely immune to external influences. He has established it as a holy of holies, a sanctum which none but the individual himself can approach.

In the depth of the inner self, each man has freedom of choice and free will. It is there that our aesthetic and moral sense resides. We can freely appreciate, judge, and discriminate. And it is on account of this freedom that God has given us the earth and made us even as little kings to rule it. It is a kind of test or trial, a rehearsal after which come the questioning and the reckoning.

In the light of the result of that test a rearrangement will take place, so that each one is put in the rank he or she has earned. We shall be called to account for the contents of that area, the inner self, the sanctum. A Prophet's tradition says:

> *Works are judged by the intentions behind them;*
> *each man will be credited with his intentions.*

The area of intention, of secret thought and feeling, is the area observed and known only to God. His reckoning will be based on the contents of that area because, as it has been mentioned, it is the area of absolute freedom. The obstacles that restrict man's freedom do not arise until man has begun to take physical action. Freedoms of individuals will then clash with one another and with the environment and society. Divine Will intervenes here to limit the scope of evil and open up possibilities for righteousness. God's mercy now comes into play to lessen the harm that people do to one another and to provide each person with powers compatible with his or her intentions.

To state that God has created a spirit for me is to state that he has created me as a free creature, that is, as a distinct individual. The two statements explain one another, and each conveys facts that are invisible, intangible, and inexpressible. Where the spirit is concerned, all expression breaks down; in fact, language can provide us with no more than hints or imprecise symbols. For here we stand on a platform outside time and outside everything that is tangible or visible.

> *They ask thee concerning the Spirit of (inspiration),*
> *Say. "The Spirit (cometh) by command of my Lord:*
> *Of knowledge it is only a little*
> *That is communicated to you (O men!)"*
> *(The Night Journey, 17: 85)*

The spirit goes to its appointed destination after death. It will be separated from us by the *Barzakh* (isthmus, barrier) until the Day of Resurrection. To the materialists of all schools, let us say what the Qur'an asks us to say:

> *Say to those who do not believe:*
> *"Do whatever ye can;*
> *We shall do our part;*
> *And wait ye! We too shall wait.*
> *To Allah do belong the unseen (secrets)*
> *Of the heavens and the earth.*
> *And to Him goeth back*
> *Every affair (for decision);*
> *Then worship Him,*
> *And put thy trust in Him;*
> *And thy Lord is not unmindful*
> *Of aught that ye do.*
> *(The Prophet Hud, 11: 121-123)*

The Spirit is an Unseen.

What happens after death is an Unseen.

All we have to offer is the tiding brought forth by our noble Prophet from the Knower of the Unseen, who sees what we see not and knows what we know not.

Chapter 12

No Clergy

The Qur'an is definite and decisive in abolishing all forms of clergy and clerical mediation. It states in many verses, clearly and unequivocally, that man has a direct contact with God and that God manages the affairs of his creatures directly without a board of directors, a Secretariat or intermediaries:

Say: "To Allah belongs
Exclusively (the right
to grant) Intercession:
To Him belongs the dominion."
(Crowds, 39: 44)

When my servants
Ask thee concerning Me,
I am indeed close (to them);
I listen to the prayer of every suppliant
When he calleth on Me.
(The Heifer, 2: 186)

We made thee not one
To watch over their doings,
Nor art thou set over them
To dispose of their affairs.
(The Cattle, 6: 107)

Thy Lord knoweth best,
Who have strayed from His Path.
And who receive guidance.
(The Bees, 16: 125)

He punisheth whom He pleaseth
And He forgiveth whom He pleaseth.
(The Repast, 5: 40)

Say: "Call upon other (gods)
Whom ye fancy, besides Allah;
They have no power –
Not the weight of an atom –
In the heavens or on earth
(Sheba, 34: 22)

God even says to His Prophet:

Whether thou ask for their forgiveness,
Or not, (their sin is unforgettable):
If thou ask seventy times
For their forgiveness,
Allah Will not forgive them;
Because they have rejected
Allah and His Messenger;
And Allah guideth not those
Who are perversely rebellious.
(Repentance, 9: 80)

Notwithstanding his high rank, his nearness to, and special relationship with God, a prophet cannot alter a divine judgment. Naturally no ordinary mortal can. It would not really matter if that mortal were an imam, a religious scholar, or even a saint. To God belongs all intercession and no mortal can intercede on behalf of another except with God's permission.

Islamic history has never known indulgences (or excommunication) on any account. "Thy Lord," God tells the Prophet, "knows very well those who have gone astray from His way, and He knows very well those who are guided." No one except God can see what a man has in the depth of his heart. Consequently, Islamic scholars were never allowed to acquire temporal power or develop into a clergy and never had any tutelage over people's destinies.

Similarly, rituals are, according to the Qur'an, simple indeed. There are five prayers a day, in the morning, at noon, afternoon, sunset, and after dusk. The regularity is meant to ensure that the believers are constantly mindful of God's presence and thus capable of averting evil. Again the physical rituals are simple: washing with water (for cleanliness and purification), bowing and kneeling to defeat a mortal's pride and remind him of his position vis-à-vis his Creator. This is a kind of psychological and physical exercise and also spiritual education. There are more complex (and harder) exercises in modern yoga that are very much in vogue among many these days, who compete in performing them willingly.

For all the simplicity of the rituals, the Qur'an has allowed them to be curtailed in case of hardship. The rites of ablution may be replaced by a simple symbolic act of *washing* the face and the hands with clean sand or dust. A person may perform his prayers sitting or lying down; he may close his eyes to imply bowing or kneeling down. The verses used at prayer may be recited silently in case of illness. Indeed the whole prayer may be a simple reminder in one's heart, without any rituals at all. Any place on earth is a mosque.

Whithersoever you turn, there is Allah's countenance.

(The Heifer, 2: 115)

Prayer (Arabic *Salah*) is a link (*Silah*) or communion. God has commanded it for the good of mankind, not for exercising His divine power. He is All-Sufficient and it is we who need Him. Prayer is our means of imbibing life, just like the sunflower imbibes life by facing the sun. By directing our faces to the source of our power, our Creator, we receive life, light, and inspiration.

Fasting is a spiritual exercise. It is a means of defeating physical desires, of controlling the animal side of man. Fasting is prescribed in all kinds of mystical exercises – Hindu, Jewish, Christian, or Buddhist. There are various forms of fasting: complete abstinence taking in nothing but water; a vegetarian diet, the exclusion of all animal foods; or, as in Islam, total fasting for a limited period every day, between dawn and sunset. Islamic fasting is the simplest.

Fasting trains the soul to endure unpleasantness and resist temptation, the basis of the ethical law. So, even if God had not ordained fasting, we would have ordained it ourselves. It is a spiritual exercise, and we need it for the development of will power, patience, and perseverance, much as our muscles need physical exercise of swimming, rowing, gymnastics, and other sports!

God allows this ordinance to be lifted in case of physical incapacity, illness or hardship. A person not fasting may redeem him or herself by feeding the poor.

The vociferous attacks on the Qur'anic penalty of amputating the hand of the thief are really baseless. In a world of murderers, an effective deterrent is needed to avert bloodshed, and in a world of unrepentant robbers, the amputation of the hand is a deterrent.

Islamic Law, however has established certain conditions and controls for carrying out this penalty. Amputation is suspended if a man steals to feed himself or if he is in dire need, even if the theft is premeditated. The penalty is applicable, to those who steal for a living, not through compulsion, but because of covetousness and greed. If a thief proves, however, to be mentally deficient or unbalanced, he must be committed for treatment in an asylum. There is also the question of the value of the stolen property. Petty thefts are usually exempt from the penalty of amputation.

The Orientalists' criticism of the Qur'an's attitude to slavery is equally baseless. The social conditions of the Arabs in pre-Islamic times precluded the freeing of all slaves at once. A revealed legislation, the Qur'an could not have decreed immediate release for fear of utter chaos. Suddenly unemployed, thousands of slaves would have been beggars on the streets. The sudden freeing of slaves would have been a catastrophe, not a solution. The Qur'an's solution was to faze out slavery. To begin with, no more slaves were to be had. The only source of slaves was the captives of war, and the Qur'an commanded that they be released or ransomed:

> *Thereafter (is the time for) either generosity or ransom.*
> *(Muhammad, 47: 4)*

No more captives would be in bondage. As for the slaves already there, they should be freed gradually. God made the freeing of a slave an established redemption for all sins, both great and small. To free a slave was made a test of man's ability to liberate his soul:

> *But he hath made no haste*
> *On the path that is steep;*
> *And what will explain*
> *To thee the path that is steep?*
> *It is freeing the bondman;*
> *(The City, 90: 11-13)*

A person's soul is liberated when he or she breaks the shackles of someone in physical bondage. The person hastens on the path that is steep, that is, he or she surmounts the biggest hurdle by conquering one's own desires. Can there be a bigger hurdle than one's own self?

The Qur'an thus put a stopper on the source of slaves and opened the way for the freeing of all already in bondage.

What happened in the days of the Umayyads Dynasty was, however, the reverse. Could it be blamed on the Qur'an? Certainly not. Theirs was a corrupt regime. The palaces of the Caliphs, aping the Persian Empire, turned into dens of sensual pleasures.

The Qur'an emphasizes in letter and spirit the brotherhood of all men, whatever their differences in color or race:

> *O mankind! reverence your Guardian Lord,*
> *Who created you from a single person,*
> *Created, of like nature,*
> *His mate, and from them twain*
> *Scattered (like seeds) countless men and women –*
> *(The Women, 4: 1)*

> *O mankind! We created you*
> *From a single (pair)*
> *Of a male and a female,*
> *And made you into*
> *Nations and tribes, that*
> *Ye may know each other*
> *(Not that ye may despise each other).*
> *Verily the most honored of you*
> *In the sight of Allah is (he who is)*
> *The most righteous of you.*
> *(The Chambers, 49: 13)*

That we worship none but Allah;
That we associate no partners with Him
(The Family of 'Imran, 3: 64)

Compared with what the Torah and the Gospel have to say about slaves, the Qur'an must be regarded as a document for the abolition of slavery. St. Peter commands slaves to obey their masters, stating that slavery is redemption for men and is designed to absolve them of the sins committed against the Lord. In his letter to the Ephesians, St. Paul says:

> *Slaves, obey your human masters with*
> *fear and trembling; and do it with a*
> *sincere heart, as though you were*
> *serving Christ.*
> *(Ephesians, 5-6)*

The Torah commands the Jews explicitly to enslave all nations other than the Israelites. In the Torah, when a city surrendered to the Jews without a fight, all the population were taken captive, both men and women became the slaves of the conquerors.

The Qur'an is in fact the only holy book that commands the unconditional freeing of all slaves. The Qur'an commands that no man shall enslave another by appointing himself as lord and master over him, that all people constitute one family descended from one father, and that no one may rise above another except by virtue of God-fearing.

The truth is that slavery as practiced by the Arabs could never be compared with the kind of human bondage established by the Europeans, where a whole people were reduced to slaves in Nazi Germany under Hitler. This is more heinous, of course, because it happened in Europe and in the twentieth century, in a time and place thought to be far removed from such acts of barbarianism.

True religion, according to the Qur'an, is a combination of faith, high morality, and good works. The emphasis on morality and ethical codes is to be found everywhere in the Qur'an.

> *Allah doth command you*
> *To render back your Trusts*
> *To those to whom they are due;*
> *And when ye judge*
> *Between man and man,*
> *That ye judge with justice*
> *(The Women, 4: 58)*

> *O ye who believe! Stand out firmly*
> *For Allah, as witnesses*
> *To fair dealing, and let not*
> *The hatred of others*
> *Toward ye make ye swerve*
> *To wrong and depart from*
> *Justice. Be just: that is*
> *Next to piety: and fear Allah*
> *For Allah is well-acquainted*
> *With all that ye do.*
> *(The Repast, 5: 8)*

> *Nor come nigh to unlawful sex*
> *For it is a shameful (deed)*
> *And an evil, opening the road*
> *(To other evils).*
> *(The Night Journey, 17: 32)*

> *And obey Allah and His Messenger*
> *And fall into no disputes,*
> *Lest ye lose heart and your power depart*
> *(The Spoils of War, 8: 46)*

Invite (all) to the Way
Of thy Lord with wisdom
And beautiful preaching;
And argue with them
In ways that are best
And most gracious
(The Bees, 16: 125)

O ye who believe!
If a wicked person comes
To you with any news,
Ascertain the truth, lest
Ye harm people unwittingly,
And afterwards become
Full of repentance for
What ye have done.
(The Chambers, 49: 6)

Those who slander chaste women,
Indiscreet but believing,
Are cursed in this life
And in the Hereafter;
For them is a grievous Penalty.
(The Light, 24: 23)

O ye who believe! Let not some men
Among you laugh at others:
It may be that the (latter) are better
Than the (former):
Nor let some women laugh at others
It may be that the (latter) are better
Than the (former):
Nor defame nor be sarcastic to each other,
Nor call each other by (offensive) nicknames:
Ill-seeming is a name connoting wickedness,

(To be used of one) after he has believed:
And those who do not desist are
(Indeed) doing wrong.
(The Chambers, 49: 11)

O ye who believe!
Enter not houses other than
Your own, until ye have
Asked permission and saluted
Those in them
(The Light, 24: 27)

And fulfill (every) engagement
For (every) engagement
Will be enquired into
(On the Day of Reckoning).
(The Night Journey, 17: 34)

O ye who believe!
Avoid suspicion as much (as possible):
For suspicion in some cases is a sin:
And spy not on each other,
Nor speak ill of each other
Behind their backs.
Would any of you like to eat
The flesh of his dead brother?
(The Chambers, 49: 12)

If one amongst the Pagans
Ask thee for asylum, grant it to him,
So that he may hear the Word of Allah;
And then escort him to where he can be secure
(Repentance, 9:6)

Regarding the ethics of, and code of conduct in war, the Qur'an gives us the best rules:

O ye who believe!
When ye meet the Unbelievers
In hostile array,
Never turn your backs to them.
(The Spoils of War , 8: 15)

God loves those who fight in His way
in ranks, as though they were a building
well-compacted.
(Those Ranged in Ranks, 37: 4)

If there are twenty amongst you,
Patient and persevering,
They will vanquish a thousand of
The Unbelievers: for these are people
Without understanding.
(The Spoils of War, 8: 65)

Say: "Running away will not profit ye
If ye are running away
From death or slaughter:
And if (ye do escape),
No more than a brief (respite)
Will ye be allowed to enjoy!"
(The Confederates, 33: 16)

Say: "Who is it that can screen you from Allah
If it be His wish to give you punishment
Or to give you mercy?
Nor will they find for themselves,
Besides Allah, any protector or helper."
(The Confederates, 33: 17)

Say: "The Death from which
Ye flee will truly overtake you:
Then will ye be sent back to
The Knower of all things,

Secret and open: and He will tell you
(The truth of) the things that ye did!"
(Friday, 62: 8)

On betrayal, the Qur'an says:

Allah sets forth, for an example
To the Unbelievers,
The wife of Noah and the wife of Lut:
They were (respectively)
Under two of our righteous servants,
But they were false to their (husbands),
And they profited nothing
Before Allah on their account,
But were told: "Enter ye the Fire
Along with (others) that enter."
(Prohibition, 66: 10)

On hypocrisy:

O ye who believe!
Why say ye that which ye do not?
Grievously odious is it in the sight of Allah
That ye say that
Which ye do not.
(The Battle Array, 61: 2-3)

The Hypocrites will be
In the lowest depths of the Fire;
No helper will thou find for them –
(The Women, 4: 145)

The Hypocrites, men and women
(Have an understanding) with each other:
They enjoin evil, and forbid
What is just, and are close
(Repentance, 9: 67)

On thrift:

By no means shall ye attain righteousness unless
Ye give (freely) of that which ye love; and whatever
Ye give of a truth Allah knoweth it well.
(The Family of 'Imran, 3: 92)

Give them preference over themselves,
Even though poverty was their (own lot)
(The Mustering, 59: 9)

Make not thy hand tied
(Like a niggard's) to thy neck,
Nor stretch it forth to its utmost reach,
So that thou become blameworthy and destitute.
(The Night Journey, 17: 29)

On conceit, humility, and kindness:

Allah loveth not the arrogant, the vainglorious –
(The Women, 4: 36)

And, out of kindness,
Lower to them the wing of humility,
And say: "My Lord! bestow on them
Thy Mercy even as they
Cherished me in childhood."
(The Night Journey, 17: 24)

On forgiveness:

Let them forgive and overlook,
Do you not wish that
Allah should forgive you?
(The Light, 24: 22)

Repel evil with that which is best:
We are well-acquainted with
The things they say.
(The Believers, 23: 96)

But indeed if any show patience and forgive,
That would truly be an exercise of courageous will
And resolution in the conduct of affairs.
(Consultation, 42: 43)

In a single comprehensive verse, these teachings are summed up:

It is not righteousness that
Ye turn your faces towards East or West;
But it is righteousness to believe in Allah
And the Last Day, and the Angels,
And the Book, and the Messengers;
To spend of your substance,
Out of love for Him,
For your kin, for orphans,
For the needy, for the wayfarer,
For those who ask,
And for the ransom of slaves;
To be steadfast in prayer,
And practice regular charity,
To fulfill the contracts which ye have made;
And to be firm and patient,
In pain (or suffering) and adversity,
(The Heifer, 2: 177)

There can be no end to examples. The Qur'an is indeed an ethical document.

Someone may object, "We don't need a Qur'an to have good character! An Englishman, far away in London, is an example of such good character without having read the Qur'an or the Bible and without believing, in fact, in any religion whatsoever!"

To raise such an objection is to fail to distinguish between two kinds of good character. The first is closer to social intelligence and masquerades as good manners. An example: an intelligent grocer discovers that good manners are good for business. As courtesy helps him to win over a customer's heart and pocket, the grocer offers friendship in order to exploit friendship. This species of good character is manufactured by a sharp, opportunistic mind. A father implants in his children good habits needed to make new friends and to succeed in business. From beginning to end, such training betrays a keen interest in this world and a desire to perfect the means of possessing it!

The other kind of morality, taught by religion, is completely different, if not indeed the opposite. A religious person believes that the world is an ephemeral business which is not worthy to be cherished; to love and meet with God is his (or her) prime target at all times. He offers love – genuine love – to everybody but expects nothing in return. He generously contributes to life in terms of money, time, and physical effort, without consideration of profit. He does it simply because of his firm belief that whatever is given away is insignificant because it is ephemeral. He does not care if this world slips through his fingers because he has his eyes set on the other. His main interest is to win the Creator, not His creatures.

A religious person is therefore capable of loving his enemy. He could even offer him advice and assistance. He can give away that which he needs; he can be charitable, however poor, and feed the hungry even when in need of the food himself. In making a contribution, he feels that the credit goes to God's Will, not to his own. In other words, he disclaims all credit for good works by attributing it all to God's kindness. This is what I would really call good character or good manners. In this sense only a believer can have good character.

A materialist or atheist can never have such character. At best, he may be well behaved. He may possess good manners owing to his social intelligence and his knowledge of the laws of profit and loss. He loves rationally and for a purpose. When he gives something away, he gives himself the credit because he does not believe in the existence of a Divine Power outside himself.

If a professed materialist can experience genuine, spiritual love; if he can give away for the sake of giving away, believing that he is not doing it for himself and therefore expecting no worldly gain from it, he must be, though without knowing it himself, a religious person deep down. He is the victim of self-delusion. One day he must, I believe, come to realize his true belonging and cast off his materialist mask. The heart is always the right indicator. It is the heart that will reveal one's true position, believer or materialist. Many are those who, formally religious, pray and fast, while their hearts are dry as summer dust and their spirits as hard as stone. Their claim to religion goes no further than the dedication rituals after their births.

On the other hand, there are many people supporting Marxist ideas while in their hearts they are utterly divorced from materialist thought and rationality. In spirit they harbor the purest sentiments imaginable as true Christians or devout Muslims but are mistaken in how they classify themselves. Perhaps they are still on the journey of discovering themselves.

Self-knowledge is often hard. Sometimes a person cannot discover the truth without struggle and suffering. The straight path of which God tells us in the Qur'an may refer to the path of suffering, that is, to man's attempt to recognize his true self and hence direct it to its Creator. It is the path taken in every journey to God from dust to the source of right and light. The beautiful words of the Qur'an are the best guide to that path.

Chapter 13

No God but God

The declaration "There is no God but God" means that nothing really exists except God. You and I are merely images that momentarily flash on the screen of existence, images on a television screen that disappear when the power is cut! When the power comes back, other images will appear only to vanish in their turn. Time, in terms of specific ages, is like that: the green vernal leaves wilt away and fall down, and the dead leaves are heaped like corpses in piles of dust. The following lines of Arabic verse are apt:

> There is many a tomb which, many times a tomb,
> Has laughed at the crowding, though parting, opposites;
> Down centuries long and ages of doom
> The relics of corpses receiving corpses –
> How dust now claims all inmates!

The very face of the earth will eventually be composed of our ancestors' bodies.

> Tread lightly! Methinks the fact of the earth
> Is made up of our own bodies.

Under a heap of dust, diggers manage to salvage a bottle of mascara (kohl phial). An archeologist eyes it with interest. "Yes, it belongs to Sit al-Mulk, sister of Al-Hakim Bi-Amrillah (a Fatimid ruler of Egypt). It is 900 years old. There's still some kohl inside." But where is Sit al-Mulk? Where is that age of hers? You could in your mind's eye see her ladies in attendance, her hairdressers, and maids of honor; you could hear the soft steps of the slave girls, and sounds of saber-rattling in the distance, a call for prayer and horses neighing. The palace *Agha* (herald) announces the arrival of an envoy from Qadish. Al-Hakim himself appears, amidst an impressive array of followers and servants.

Where is all this?

Under a heap of dust; it has become dust itself. It was a dream in time's own mind. Tomorrow you and I will go under the heap of dust. Our age will be reduced to a single line in a nook, a dream in the mind of a historian. Diggers will discover your momentos under the dust, and from them archeologists will reconstruct truth, the One Living Eternal Presence.

Truly thou wilt die (one day),
And truly they (too) will die (one day).
(Crowds, 39:30)

Wake up to reality. You do not exist! You are but a shadow and shadow-like you exist for as long as the sun is up in the sky! Once set, you'll disappear together with all the shadows that had stretched out by your side! Your existence is derivative and therefore unreal. You live on a supply from God so that if the supply is held up, you will cease to exist.

God exists independently of everything else. He is All Sufficient – the only existing reality, and therefore, there is no god but He.

Everything has its source in Him and goes back to Him. He is the only everlasting reality; everything else is a passing shadow. God sends down revelation to Muhammad:

Know, therefore, that there is no god but
Allah, and ask forgiveness for thy fault.
(Muhammad, 47: 19)

He doth send down His angels
With inspiration of His Command,
To such of His servants
As He pleaseth (saying):
"Warn (Man) that there is no god
But I: so do your duty unto Me."
(The Bees, 16: 2)

That there is no god but God is the first and most important tiding from heaven and is the heart of the Qur'an, the heart of Islam, and the heart of all creeds. Hence the Prophet's tradition:

While the Unbelievers got up in their hearts
Heat and cant – the heat and cant of Ignorance –
Allah sent down His Tranquillity to His Messenger
And to the Believers, and made them
Stick close to the command of self-restraint;
And well were they entitled to it and worthy of it.
And Allah has full knowledge of all things.
(The Victory, 48: 26)

"There is no god but God" is the angels' incantation in the Higher Assembly, as they sing the glories of God.

It is the testimony that Muslims recite a dozen times a day at prayer. It is the word of salvation uttered by the happy person in the throes of death before giving up his or her soul. It warns that everything will perish. This world is but a designer's set, a house of cards, a toy city. It is doomed and will be dismantled and repacked.

If made a constitution for life, these words are capable of charting out a better, truer, and more honest life wherein nothing counts apart from eternal values that are established by the Creator.

"There is no god but God" means that we will worship none

but God. We are not going to worship one another; we are not going to have gods from among ourselves. Nothing will make us fight one another because nothing, we now know, really exists.

We shall not be vain, knowing that we are merely shadows playing on the face of the water. We shall not be overjoyed by wealth or over saddened by poverty. We shall not hesitate to make sacrifices or be horrified by disasters, knowing that they are but transitory conditions. This fact alone inspires us to endure the severest pains, for pains like pleasures are transient.

We shall not be afraid. How can a dead man fear death? We shall not fear one another, when each one of us knows that he is no more than a scarecrow designed to drive away the scavengers who try to peck away at our souls.

We shall love and give away in humility. We shall resist and fight bravely. We shall receive our laurels in shyness, and in shyness listen to the words of praise.

We shall have infinite fortitude and make endless sacrifices. We shall not fear war, the bomb, microbes or illness, because we know that the source is One, that they all come from God and are merely the instruments of enacting His Will. A microbe cannot in itself be harmful because both harm and benefit come from God and it is God that designs and determines all. It is God who created the scorpion, poison, and the rose; it is He who spreads the fragrance in the air and the poison in the veins. He is the Giver of Life and Death. His pre-ordination cannot be altered, and His command cannot be modified. He is the only doer and we are only His means.

Our hearts will be filled with tranquility, peace, and security as we realize that all sustenance is derived from the Living God, the Immortal.

When a person believes in God as the Ultimate and Omnipotent, he or she will of necessity rely on God's help and repose his or her trust in Him. This reliance or trust (*tawakkul*) is a positive quality; it must be distinguished from the negative tawaakul.

Positive trust in God (*tawakkul*) means that a person must have the needed resolve to accomplish a given task before undertaking it. He or she must do his or her best, and believe that God will determine the ultimate result. He or she must make the necessary effort, though the success or failure of that effort, he or she believes, is preordained.

> *Then, when thou hast taken a decision,*
> *Put thy trust in Allah*
> *(The Family of 'Imran, 3: 159)*

A *mutawakkil*, one who puts his (or her) trust in God, differs from the proud man in that the former denies himself any intrinsic power. He fulfills his task but ascribes his success to God's will not to his own ability. He regards his success as help from God not a personal achievement. He knows that the work of his own hands is only one of the instruments employed by God to secure success.

On the other hand, the proud person thinks that his (or her) achievements are solely due to his intelligence, efforts, and cleverness. He cannot conceive of any other will than his own whether within his personal life or in the universe.

A *mutawaakil*, a person who passively relies on God, differs from both. He (or she) lacks will power and resolve and, without lifting a finger, expects God to do everything for him. He is like certain Jews who, when Moses called on them to fight, answered:

"Go thou, and thy Lord,
And fight ye two,
While we sit here (and watch)."
(The Repast, 5: 24)

While the mutawakkil puts his trust in himself and in God, the passive mutawaakil neither trusts himself nor believes in the order established by God, an order wherein the chain of causes and effects is the basic pillar. Nothing can be achieved, according to that order, without the necessary resolve and effort.

An example of the positive mutawakkil is the person who, having decided to travel to Alexandria, buys himself a ticket, reserves a seat, promptly does his packing, and catches the train on time. Once in his seat, he leaves the rest to the driver. He puts his trust in the driver's ability and the laws governing the motion of the locomotive. He is so assured and so trusting in fact that he now goes to sleep. If he behaves differently, if he runs in panic, for instance, to the driver to make sure that he drives well, he will be regarded as a fool. He would be meddling in other people's affairs.

The world is like that train on which we are the travelers. We try to get ourselves the best seats, but trust the driver and the laws of motion. We trust in God, more clever than any mortal driver, and we trust in His laws which we know, from our observations of the universe, to be perfect.

As we work hard, sparing no effort in trying to ensure success, our hearts are warmed up by such trust. Our souls will enjoy the tranquility of trust, and our minds will be assured that justice will take its course and that each one of us will get what he or she deserves. Consequently, we are never saddened by failure and never vain in success. If we panicked or were distressed by any untoward occurrences (which are in reality preordained), we would be displaying a lack of trust in the ability of the driver.

The passively dependent mutawaakil is a different kind of traveler. He thinks of travel but lacks the necessary resolve: he neither books a seat nor does his packing. He tells you he believes in God, and relies on Him, and that He will consequently send him the tickets from Heaven, perhaps, or send someone along to give him a free lift. This kind of person will end up, of course, where he is. He will blame his failure on God, or will tell you that it is God's will and that he therefore accepts it because he is a believer. His actions do not, however, show any real belief because to believe in God is to believe in the order established by Him in this world – the order of cause and effect where resolve and effort constitute the necessary means of fulfilling any task. God has commanded us most emphatically to work:

> And say: "Work (righteousness):
> Soon will Allah observe your work
> (Repentance, 9: 105)

To be a true mutawakkil is to attain a high rank indeed. Only a devout believer (not to say a mystic) is capable of it, because the point of departure is the belief that there is no god but God, that there is no omnipotent except God.

A true mutawakkil trusts God, loves Him, and loves His order. He accepts the responsibilities and the burdens established by God as prerequisites for success. He does not shirk duty and does his utmost, but also surrenders himself all the while to God's will. He does not care whether his effort will succeed or not because he is sure that in the end he will get what he deserves. He knows that God is the Fair Judge who does injustice to nobody. When he succeeds, he resists the vanity of success and denies that it was due to his power. He says in humility, "I could not have done this unless God had wanted it. God had provided the necessary means of attaining my target, the means being both my work and myself. Praise be to God!" If he fails, he would not change heart, show any regret or cry over defeat. He would say confidently, "God has given me what is right for me."

> But it is possible that ye dislike a thing
> Which is good for you, and that ye love a thing
> Which is bad for you.
> But Allah knoweth, and ye know not.
>
> (The Heifer, 2: 216)

He (or she) remembers and reminds himself all the time that he does not know what God alone knows, and that consequently he should not object to God's will. He always returns to God and trusts in Him even as he does his best to achieve success, believing this to be the law of God. For him, "There is no god but God" is not a group of words nicely put together but a way of life and a law of heart. It has become his guide, the only light in the dark world about him. He therefore denies at every step any intrinsic power and believe all power to come from God because nothing really exists apart from God; there can be no power apart from His. Such is true piety.

It has been suggested that "There is no god but God" is the word of the God-fearing because it makes one really and truly God-fearing. He (or she) who says it and assimilates its meaning in his or her heart and mind, so that it becomes the beacon lighting his or her way, will have captured the true spirit of religion.

In a Qudsi verse, God says:

> "There is no god but God" is my bastion.
> He who says it is admitted;
> and he who is admitted
> will be secure from My chastisement.

It is the opening statement in all incantations. Before singing the glories of God, the mystics start by uttering it, as the means of establishing God's real existence, that is, that He alone exists in reality while all other phenomena are illusions.

He is the Living, the Everlasting; He gives life to all, takes His life from none.

He is the light with which we see things; the light of the eye, the light of the heart and the mind.

He is the Truth; all else is untruth.

He is the Transcendent; He fills up Earth and the heavens but transcends them; He is never defined in terms of space and time.

He is the infinitely powerful, infinitely present.

He is the only One to whom you could turn for succor; you could turn to none else.

Glory be to Him; hallowed be His name; glory be to the Being that rises above description.

Like Him there is naught in Heaven or on Earth.

The eyes attain Him not, but He attains the eyes.

He has not begotten, and has not been begotten, and equal to Him is no one.

Too great is God to have a spouse or offspring.

How can He be in need of offspring when He is the Creator and Maker of all beings? He is the All-Sufficient, the Almighty, the Omnipotent, who rules each and all.

He originates Creation, and then brings it back again, using a single word of command. The sea would be spent before the words of my Lord are spent.

He is veiled from us by being too radiant; He is not to be seen because He is only too present; He is hidden by being too conspicuous.

The beginning is in Him; the return is to Him.

There can be no peace except in His company; no tranquility except in His Being.

He is our Lord and Master; He encompasses everything in Knowledge and Mercy.

We have failed to appreciate His power, and we cannot do it even if we tried. How could we praise Him rightly when we know so little of His work, His knowledge, or His Creation? We can hardly aspire to do so. And that is why He has praised Himself in al-Fatihah, the opening chapter of His Book, "Praise belongs to God, the Lord of all Being."

He is All-Praiseworthy because He alone exists in truth, while we are the evidence of His generosity. He alone is capable of praise because He alone knows the hidden fruits of His creative power. What we see is merely a single atom, the Earth moving about in heavens without horizons.

So it is this form of praise that is accepted by the All-Gentle, the All-Generous. We whisper it at the beginning of every prayer, "Praise belongs to God, Lord of all Being."

He teaches us that He created the world in His Name as the All-Merciful, the All-Compassionate, and not in His Name as the Omnipotent, the All-Compeller. In other words, He created the world with mercy, with absolute mercy ("All-Merciful" implies showing absolute mercy to all creatures, those who deserve it and those who do not.) We start everything we do by saying "In the Name of God, the Merciful, the Compassionate," because it was in His name as All-Merciful, All-Compassionate, that creation started. Everything came into being through mercy not compulsion. He made mercy a quality that belongs to Him. In a Qudsi Verse He says:

My mercy comes before My wrath.

The Fatihah (opening chapter of the Qur'an) has the epithets "All-Merciful, All-Compassionate" before the "Master of the Day of Doom," that day being the day of wrath when man will be condemned by the work of his own hands.

"There is no god but God" implies absolute monotheism. In the Fatihah there are beautiful verses which direct attention to the One God:

> Thee do we worship and Thine aid we seek.
> Show us the straight way.
> (The Opening, 1: 5-6)

We worship Him alone, ask help from Him because He alone truly exists; and we ask Him to guide our steps to the straight path because He alone is capable of it. The straight path leads to God, to the Truth and Salvation.

The Fatihah is a chapter that tells us about God and the path leading to Him in seven brief verses so eloquent that they sum up the contents of the entire Qur'an. The Qur'an is essentially a book that tells us about God, the Hereafter, and the path leading to Him.

God in the Qur'an is an entity with names, epithets, and actions. The actions can be seen in God's creation — the heavens, the earth, the living world, and the Unseen. The Heaven and Hell, and the other world are His creation too. According to the Qur'an, the way to God is through worship, God's law, and love. This is the straight path leading to safety. The Fatihah, as we have seen, sums up these facts and presents them in seven concordant verses, almost like a symphony with a beautiful divine melody. Our Prophet says that the Fatihah is the best chapter of the Qur'an, that the Verse of the Chair is the Master verse, and the Yaseen chapter is the heart of the Qur'an.

An intelligent reading of the Qur'an will reveal that the secret lies in the dictum, "There is no god but God"; it is the seed which grew into the fruit-laden tree of the whole book. Belief in One God is at the root of our vast information and various branches of knowledge.

Now look at the magnificent Verse of the Chair that opens with the statement of monotheism, then proceeds to establish the epithets of the One Eternal Living God:

> Allah! There is no god But He – the Living,
> The Self-subsisting, Eternal.
> No slumber can seize Him nor sleep.
> His are all things in the heavens and on earth.
> Who is there that can intercede in
> His presence except as He permitteth?
> He knoweth what (appeareth to His Creatures as)
> Before or after or behind them.
> Nor shall they compass aught of His knowledge
> Except as He willeth. His Throne doth extend
> Over the heavens and the earth,
> And He feeleth
> No fatigue in guarding
> And preserving them
> For He is the Most High,
> The Supreme (in glory).
> (The Heifer, 2: 255)

Many chapters and verses in the Qur'an start or end or lead to the statement of monotheism. Everything begins with recognition of the One God and goes ultimately to it. From rudimentary arithmetic we know that an integer may be divided indefinitely to give us all fractions, numbers, and parts thereof; but the Integer that is God gives us all the numbers without being capable of division;

thus the Arabic epithet *Ahad* that is often combined with the Arabic for *one* (*Wahid*) to mean *the Indivisible One*. *Ahad* refers to an integer that cannot be conceivably approached in terms of fractions; a whole that does not consist of parts or organs but is always a whole. This explains why one of God's most beautiful names is Peace, *Salaam* (often rendered "All-Peaceable").

No individual can hope to achieve internal peace until he has realized inner unity through harmony. His desires, his mind, his will, and his targets must of course be in harmony; but that is not enough. They should constitute an integer, an indivisible entity; that is only possible through unity with God. Man may be made one with God in a mystical sense, that is, when he puts his feet on the straight path leading to God. To attain universal peace, we too must unite states, nations, and sects.

Chapter 14

The Miracle of the Qur'an

The Qur'an is full of prophecies. Some of these were realized during the lifetime of Muhammad, but others will not be realized until much later, at a preappointed time.

Before the Battle of Badr, when a few Muslims fought a huge army of infidels, revelation came down with good tidings which came to pass:

Behold! Allah promised you
One of the two (enemy) parties,
That it should be yours
(The Spoils of War, 8: 7)

Soon will their multitude be put to flight,
And they will show their backs.
(The Moon, 54: 45)

Before the conquest of Makkah, when the return to Makkah had seemed an unattainable dream to the Muslims in Medina (where they had been staying as émigrés), revelation came down to confirm the Prophet's vision which came to pass:

Truly did Allah fulfill the vision for His Messenger:
Ye shall enter the Sacred Mosque, if Allah wills,
With mind secure, heads shaved, hair cut short
And without fear. For He knew what ye knew not,
And He granted besides this, a speedy victory.
(The Victory, 48: 27)

When the army of the Roman Empire was defeated (by the Persians), revelation came down to Muhammad presaging victory soon to come:

> The Roman Empire has been defeated –
> In a land close by: but they (even) after
> (This) defeat of theirs, will soon be victorious –
> Within a few years.
> With Allah is the Decision,
> In the Past and in the Future
> On that Day shall the Believers rejoice –
> (The Romans 30: 2-4)

The Arabic word for *few* normally denotes anything between three and nine; the Romans were actually victorious seven years after their defeat. Let us also consider the promise to the Israelites, where the Qur'an addresses the Jews:

> And We gave (clear) warning
> To the children of Israel in the Book
> That twice would they do mischief
> On the earth and be elated
> With mighty arrogance
> (The Night Journey, 17: 4)

Israel was riding high for the second time, waxing insolent in her attempt to realize her dream of conquering all the lands between the Nile and Euphrates rivers. But, being on the crest of a wave, she must, as the Qur'an says, fall into a trough of defeat.

There are other prophecies in the Qur'an. Some of these will warn us of the nearing Day of Doom, such as the splitting of the moon and the rising of the smoke.

When the Qur'an argues, it uses simple reasoning but allows no loopholes to mar its case. Of the infidel who does not believe that he will be resurrected, the Qur'an says:

And he makes comparisons
For Us, and forgets his own (origin) and creation
He says, "Who can give life to (dry) bones
And decomposed ones (at that)?"
Say, "He will give them life
Who created them for the first time
For He is well versed
In every kind of creation!–
(Yaseen, 36: 78-79)

Were We then weary with the first Creation,
That they should be in confused doubt
About a new Creation?
(Qaf, 50: 15)

To prove the existence of the Creator, the Qur'an does not offer us pages of glib philosophical arguments but simply asks a question that confounds the infidels:

Were they created of nothing?
Or were they themselves the creators?
(The Mount, 52: 35)

The issue raised by these rhetorical questions has survived five thousand years of philosophizing and the questions remain rhetorical.

To explain the elementary philosophical fact that there is for everything an ephemeral appearance and a lasting essence, the Qur'an does not weave webs of logical arguments or set traps of clever deductions as the professional philosophers are wont to do. It simply leads to the truth by striking a similitude:

The scum disappears like froth cast out;
While that which is for the good
Of mankind remains on the earth.
Thus doth Allah set forth parables.
(The Thunder, 13: 17)

And to silence all opposition, the Qur'an strikes another similitude:

> O men! Here is a parable set forth!
> Listen to it! Those on whom, besides Allah,
> Ye call, cannot create (even) a fly,
> If they all met together for the purpose!
> And if the fly should snatch away anything from them,
> They would have no power to release it from the fly.
> Feeble are those who petition and those whom they petition!
> (The Pilgrimage, 22: 73)

This is an instance of man's weakness that cannot be rebutted, and a thousand years of scientific and technological development has hardly changed the situation. For who can create a fly — small, weak, and insignificant though it is? If a fly robs you of your life, by giving you a disease, who can restore your life? Indeed, if a fly robs you of a single particle of starch (picked up from your food), the chemical geniuses of the world will be helpless to recover it from the fly's guts, as the starch will be instantly metabolized by the digestive enzymes and turned into sugar! Feeble indeed alike are the seeker and the sought! Feeble are the chemical human wizards, the fly, and the starch particle, especially as seen against the vastness of this intractable world and infinite galaxies.

Inimitable and enigmatic in its simplicity, the Qur'an deals with the most complex questions, and gets them across to the simplest minds.

Like the body, the soul is, according to the Qur'an, mortal:

> Every soul shall taste of death
> (The Family of 'Imran, 3: 185)

> Nor can a soul die except by Allah's leave
> (The Family of 'Imran, 3: 145)

Take not life, which Allah hath made sacred,
Except by way of justice and law
(The Cattle, 6: 151)

In the Qur'an, the soul may mean the sum total of desires, instincts, and passions:

The (human) soul is certainly prone to evil
(The Prophet Joseph, 12: 53)

Thus did my soul suggest to me
(Ta Ha, 20: 96)

It may also mean a transcendent reproachful soul:

I do call to witness the Resurrection Day
And I do call to witness
The self-reproaching spirit (eschew evil)
(The Resurrection, 75: 1-2)

It is used in other contexts to imply the immortal spirit of man:

It is Allah that takes
The souls (of men) at death
And those that die not
(He takes) during their sleep.
(Crowds, 39: 42)

As used in the Qur'an, the spirit is a mystery, a divine secret. It is immortal and God takes it unto himself:

They ask thee concerning the Spirit (of inspiration)
Say: "The Spirit (cometh) by command of my Lord:
Of knowledge it is only a little that is communicated
To you (O men!)
(The Night Journey, 17: 85)

In philosophy, the spirit is no less a mystery. On the basis of tangible evidence no decisive proof of its existence may be furnished, but then it would be arbitrary to deny it and ignorant to disregard the question altogether. It is a most insuperable problem, and our limited knowledge is simply helpless to find a satisfactory solution for it. It is much more difficult than that of God's existence.

We need hardly sum up what the Qur'an has to say about many other important questions to show how inimitable it is. We have already reviewed the basic Qur'anic ideas on the Story of Creation, on responsibility and worship.

To show the inimitability of the Qur'an, writers often adduce that the Qur'an includes many prophecies regarding the future of mankind, reports on certain dim and distance patches of human history, information now proven correct in the light of modern science (after the lapse of a thousand years), and perfect solutions for many problems pertaining to government, ethics, law, and metaphysics.

However, I believe that the inimitability of the Qur'an is primarily due to the mysterious feeling it evokes in the reader's heart by the unique arrangement of the words. It is a beautiful symphony played without instruments, enchanting poetry without meter, rhyme or rhythm. Listen to what Zechariah says to his Lord:

> Behold! he cried to his Lord in secret,
> Praying: "O my Lord!
> Infirm indeed are my bones,
> And the hair of my head
> Doth glisten with grey:
> But never am I unblest, O my Lord,
> In my prayer to Thee!"
> (Mary, 19: 3-4)

Consider the words of Christ as a babe in the arms of his mother:

> He said: "I am indeed a servant of Allah;
> He hath given me Revelation
> And made me a prophet;
> And He hath made me
> Blessed wheresoever I be,
> And hath enjoined on me
> Prayer and Charity as long as I live."
> (Mary, 19: 30-31)

The following sentence describes the humility of the Messengers:

> Whenever the Signs
> Of (Allah) Most Gracious
> Were rehearsed to them,
> They would fall down
> In prostrate adoration
> And in tears.
> (Mary, 19: 58)

Here sounds the awful note characteristic of the encounter with God on the Day of Resurrection:

> (All) faces shall be humbled
> Before (Him) – the Living,
> The Self-Subsisting, Eternal:
> Hopeless indeed will be
> The man that carries
> Iniquity (on his back).
> (Ta Ha, 20: 111)

Consider the divine music of the Arabic words of the opening verses of Ta Ha. Though impossible to adequately render in English, here is what God tells his prophet Muhammad:

Ta Ha
We have not sent down the Qur'an to thee
To be (an occasion) for thy distress,
But only as an admonition
To those who fear (Allah) –
A revelation from Him who created the earth
And the heavens on high.
(Allah) Most Gracious is firmly established
On the throne (of authority)
To Him belongs what is in the heavens and on earth,
And all between them, and all beneath the soil.
If thou pronounce the word (aloud),
(It is no matter) for verily He knoweth
What is secret and what is yet more hidden.
Allah! there is no god but He!
To Him belong the Most Beautiful Names.
(Ta Ha, 20: 1-8)

Turning to report on the infidels and the harsh punishment inflicted on them, the Qur'an uses tunes reminiscent of brass instruments, harsh and grating, and the Arabic words sound more like solid pieces of rock:

For We sent against them
A furious wind, on a Day
Of violent Disaster,
Plucking out men as if
They were roots of palm-trees
Torn up (from the ground).
(The Moon, 54: 19-20)

When the angels sing the glories of God and ask Him to grant the believers forgiveness, the Qur'anic words flow like liquid gold.

Our Lord!
Thy Reach is over all things
In Mercy and Knowledge.
Forgive, then, those who
Turn in Repentance, and follow
The Path; and preserve them
From the Penalty
Of the Blazing Fire!
(Forgiver of Sins, 40: 7)

Turning in the same chapter to the Day of Doom, terror and horror seem to rear their ugly heads; the words and sentences are quite tense:

Warn them of the Day
That is (ever) drawing near,
When the Hearts will
(Come) right up to the Throats
To choke (them);
No intimate friend, nor intercessor
Will the wrongdoers have
Who could be listened to.
(Forgiver, 40: 18)

Then comes expostulation when it is too late:

O man! what has seduced thee from
Thy Lord Most Beneficient?–
Him Who created thee,
Fashioned thee in due proportion,
And gave thee a just bias;
In whatever Form He wills,
Does He put thee together.
(The Cleaving Asunder, 82: 6-8)

Enjoy the good tidings as the angels tell Mary about her immi-
nent bearing of Jesus:

> *Behold! the angels said:*
> *"O Mary! Allah giveth thee*
> *Glad tidings of a Word*
> *From Him: his name*
> *Will be Christ Jesus.*
> *The son of Mary, held in honor*
> *In this world and the Hereafter*
> *And of (the company of) those*
> *Nearest to Allah...*
> *And Allah will teach him*
> *The Book and Wisdom*
> *The Law and the Gospel*
> *(The Family of 'Imran, 3: 45, 48)*

In the following passages, the screeching noise of the Arabic
word for *deafening, Saakhhah,* seems to cut as sharp as a knife:

> *At length, when there*
> *Comes the Deafening Noise–*
> *That Day shall a man*
> *Flee from his own brother*
> *And from his mother and his father.*
> *And from his wife and his children.*
> *Each of them, that Day,*
> *Will have enough concern (of his own)*
> *To make him indifferent to the others.*
> *(He Frowned, 80: 33-37)*

There are variations, coloring, and juxtaposition of the Arabic
sounds in a unique structure that is comparable to nothing ever
written before or after the Qur'an. The amazing thing is that it
all appears so easy and simple. You could never feel any effects of
workmanship because no complexities or clever literary tricks mar

the text. The words flow so easily and smoothly into one's heart to arouse the enigmatic feeling of piety before the mind wakes up to analyze the meaning, to meditate on and ponder the thoughts. The mere entry of the word into the ear means that it has reached the heart, engendering that feeling which I find inscrutable. This quality of the Qur'anic sentence, apart from all other qualities, makes the Qur'an an inexplicable phenomenon among all known literary genres.

The most any author or man of letters can hope to do is express himself, offer insights into one's self and his or her society, deal with well known historical facts, or predict the future on the basis of present indications, in a poem, a novel or a play. The Qur'an, however, is different from all this: it relates facts from unrecorded history, future events not borne out by the present, and scientific facts as yet undiscovered. It deals with the unseen with facts shrouded in absolute mystery. True, some mystics are allowed by God to know a few of these mysteries revealed to them, but they come to confirm what the Qur'an has already told us.

Besides, the Qur'an gives eternal words of wisdom, a constitution for an ideal life, a philosophy of ethics, judgment, theology, metaphysics, business dealings, marriage, companionship, war, peace, and worship, in a unique style of unprecedented and unequalled aesthetic qualities which can be found neither in poetry nor in poetic prose. Unprecedented, we say, but it has never and can never be equaled to the end of time.

> And if ye are in doubt
> As to what We have revealed
> From time to time to Our servant,
> Then produce a Surah like thereunto;
> And call your witnesses or helpers
> (If there are any) besides Allah,

If your (doubts) are true.
And if ye cannot–
And of a surety ye cannot–
Then fear the Fire whose fuel is Men and Stones–
Which is prepared for those who reject Faith.
(The Heifer, 2: 23-24)

The Qur'an thus challenges us to produce even a single surah in imitation of it, then proceeds to state with certainty that we won't be able to do so. The Qur'an actually states something that has been confirmed down through the centuries. Over 1400 years, no single imitation of the Qur'an has survived, in spite of the fact that numerous enemies and enviers of Islam have tried their hands at it. Indeed, the challenge stands even today; and the Qur'an never ceases to reveal its secrets, confirming its inimitability.

Soon will We show them
Our Signs in the (furthest)
Regions (of the earth), and
In their own souls, until
It becomes manifest to them
That this is the Truth.
(Expounded, 41: 53)

This is another challenge: the future will confirm the truth of certain verses (the word for both "signs" and "verses" in Arabic is *Ayat*) that we still regard as enigmatic, as pertaining to the Unseen.

Do they not consider
The Qur'an (with care)?
Had it been from other
Than Allah, they would surely
Have found therein much discrepancy.
(The Women, 4: 82)

A major feature of the Qur'an is its perfect structure. Apart from syntactical contingencies, no word is placed before or after another without reason. Take the fact that the habitual order of "sight and sound" is reversed in many verses. Physiologists have today explained away this mystery. The auditory mechanism in man, they tell us, is more advanced, more complex, and more delicate than the visual mechanism. The ear is superior to the eye in being capable of perceiving abstractions such as musical structures, and dovetailed notation, as happens in polyphony, even while distinguishing each tune separately. A mother can distinguish her baby's crying amidst a host of interfering sounds. It all happens in a fraction of a second, of course. The eye is, on the contrary, often deluded by the crowding details; the son is lost to his mother's eye, never to her ear; and as for the visual equivalent of music, don't we often hear of a man who "cannot see the forest for the trees"? Moses heard God's words, but could never see him! Science provides us today with many proofs of the superiority of hearing over vision.

Though such scientific discoveries had not been made in the days when the Qur'an was revealed, hearing is made to precede vision so conspicuously in verses dealing with more than seventeen subjects.

> When ye knew nothing; and He
> Gave you hearing and sight
> And intelligence and affection;
> That ye may give thanks (to Allah).
> (The Bees, 16: 78)

> Who is it that has power over hearing
> And sight? And who is it that brings out
> The living from the dead
> And the dead from the living?
> (The Prophet Jonah [Yunus], 10: 31)

And We have endowed them
With (faculties of) hearing, seeing,
Heart and intellect
(Winding Sand-tracts, 46: 26)

At length, when they reach the (Fire),
Their hearing, their sight, and their skins
Will bear witness against them,
As to (all) their deeds.
(Expounded, 41: 20)

How plainly will they hear
And see, the Day that
They will appear before us
(Mary, 19: 38)

It is He Who has created
For you (the faculties of)
Hearing, sight, feeling
And understanding: little thanks
It is ye give!
(The Believers, 23: 78)

Every act of hearing, or of seeing
Or of (feeling in) the heart
Will be enquired into
(On the Day of Reckoning).
(The Night Journey, 17: 36)

Ye did not seek to hide yourselves, lest
Your hearing, your sight,
And your skins should bear
Witness against you!
(Expounded, 41: 22)

Say: "Think ye, if Allah took away
Your hearing and your sight..."
(The Cattle, 6: 46)

And if Allah willed, He could take away
Their faculty of hearing and seeing;
For Allah hath power over all things.
(The Heifer, 2: 20)

Those are they whose hearts,
Ears, and eyes Allah has sealed up
And they take no heed.
(The Bees, 16: 108)

The fact that the heart preceded both senses confirms that the order is one of superiority.

And We had endowed them with (faculties of)
Hearing, seeing, heart and intellect:
But of no profit to them
(Winding Sand-tracts, 46: 26)

Such are the men whom Allah has cursed
For He has made them deaf and blinded their sight.
(Muhammad, 47: 23)

Allah is He Who heareth and seeth all things.
(The Women, 4: 58)

Verily We created human from a drop
Of mingled sperm, in order to try him:
So We gave him (the gifts), of Hearing and Sight.
(The Human, 76: 2)

There is nothing whatever like unto Him,
And He is the One that hears and sees (all things).
(Consultation, 42: 11)

> *Allah (always) hears the arguments between*
> *both sides among you:*
> *For Allah hears and sees (all things).*
> *(The Woman Who Pleads, 58: 1)*

Repeatedly and quite deliberately, the Qur'an puts hearing before sight, although the latter is commonly held in greater esteem, and although physiology and anatomy, which today establish the superiority of hearing, were not known at the time.

What we have here is, therefore, a perfect arrangement of the words and consummate precision and accuracy — "A Book whose verses are perfect," wherein no word is made to precede or follow another without reason. Sometimes the choice of a word to fit the expression is a miracle of eloquence in itself:

> *And We send the fecundating winds,*
> *That cause the rain to descend*
> *From the sky, therewith providing you*
> *With water (in abundance)*
> *Though ye are not*
> *The guardians of its stores!*
> *(El Hijr, 15: 22)*

The use of fertilizing as an epithet for the wind calls for a patient examination. The cold wind gathers clouds, and drives the electrically charged clouds to an encounter in the sky where the negatively charged clouds meet the positively charged ones, with ensuing lightning, thunder and rain. Does this not resemble fertilization? The metaphoric copulation of clouds produces lightning, thunder and rain! The ion-charged rain fertilizes the earth in a different fashion (another metaphoric copulation between water and earth). The wind also carries the pollen from one flower to another to complete another cycle of fertilization, a literal fertilization this time! The scientific information regarding electrically charged clouds and the transfer of pollen was unheard of when the verse was revealed.

Qur'anic commentators have noted the metaphoric sense of the word *fecundating (fertilizing)* but stopped there, explaining that the wind carries the clouds and causes rain to fertilize the earth, so, the wind is no more than a metaphoric fertilizer. But science opens up to us the treasures of eloquence within this word: it now turns out to be true, literally and metaphorically, in part and in whole. To put it where it belongs in the verse is a miracle, no less, of precision and perfection characteristic of Qur'anic eloquence.

This is therefore an expression that is both literally and metaphorically true: whichever way you look at it, you'll find it to be true. Besides, it is a new and unusual epithet for the wind. Aesthetically it is simply superb, and the Arabic sound of it is unsurpassable: *We loosed the wind, fertilizing.* You read it aloud and your ear is held in enchantment and admiration.

Let us take another example:

> *The parable of those who*
> *Take protectors other than Allah*
> *Is that of the Spider,*
> *Who builds (to itself) a home;*
> *But truly the flimsiest of homes*
> *Is the Spider's home –*
> *If they but knew.*
> *(The Spider, 29: 41)*

The most striking detail is the reference to the "home" of the spider, not its web. It must be significant and must have an explanation. Science tells us today that a single strand of a spider's web is three times stronger than a comparable thread of steel, and much stronger and more flexible than a comparable one of silk. A web must be, therefore, more than adequate considering the limited requirements of the spider; the web should constitute (for the purposes of serving the spider) an impregnable castle. Why should the Qur'an say that surely the frailest of homes is the home of the spider, then hasten to add, "if they but knew"? There must be a reason.

There is in fact a biological secret which modern science has recently revealed that the spider's home is far from being a home in the sense of being safe and secure. The female spider weaves the web and is the ruler there; she kills the male immediately after mating and devours him. The litter eat one another after hatching. If lucky enough, the male runs away the minute he mates with the female and never tries to set foot in her home again!

Apart from this, the female spider prepares her home to be a trap, designed to catch any insect that touches it. Any visitors to that home are killed and devoured instantly.

Hardly a home, then, is it! It is more like a slaughter house where fear and anguish reign. It is the frailest home to anyone seeking refuge. The Arabic word for *flimsy* [*Wahan*] has connotations of extreme suffering and definite plight which applies to those who seek others apart from God for protection, help, and support:

> *"But truly the flimsiest of houses*
> *Is the Spider's house —"*
> *(The Spider, 29: 41)*

The entire passage is perfection itself, a precise expression, hidden meaning, rightly placed words and secrets revealed by science a thousand years after the Prophet's death. This is no doubt a miracle that the mind can explain in no other way than by attributing it to a divine source – God.

In another surah (chapter), we hear of the period of time spent by the cave-sleepers in the cave:

> So they stayed in their Cave
> Three hundred years, and (some)
> Add nine (more).
> (The Cave, 18: 25)

We know now, using astronomical reckoning, that the three hundred years in the solar calendar are equal to 309 years in the lunar (calculated to the day, hour and minute). As the calendar used when the verse was revealed was lunar, the Qur'an made this adjustment, the extra nine years being the difference. This remained a secret for a long time and has only been revealed recently.

Let us take another example:

> Does man think that We
> Cannot assemble his bones?
> Nay, We are able to put
> Together in perfect order
> The very tips of his fingers.
> (The Resurrection, 75: 3-4)

God says this in the context of challenge, pointing out that the miracle of shaping the finger and bringing it back to life in its original form is greater than that of reviving dead bones. This is a fact which became known to man only a thousand years after that verse was revealed. Each individual has his own individual fingerprints which are not shared by any other person. Not even identical twins have the same fingerprints.

In another surah, the Qur'an says:

> *By the Firmament*
> *Which returns (in its round),*
> *And by the Earth which opens out*
> *For the gushing of springs*
> *Or the sprouting of vegetation) –*
> *(The Night Star, 86: 11-12)*

The Qur'an says that the heaven returns what goes up to it (for example, water vapor returns to us in the form of rain). We know now that the transmission of radio and television programs is based on the same principle: radiation is directed at the ionosphere, up in the sky, before it is reflected back to earth. That is why we can receive radio transmissions from far off lands. With the sky acting like a mirror, it can easily be described as a returning agent. It also returns infrared rays to keep the earth warm. So, God may vow by the heaven and what it returns to us.

The earth is described as splitting; it splits up to let out plants, natural gas, petroleum, mineral water jets, and volcano lava, and it splits literally with every earth tremor. Once again, we have precise terms with comprehensive meanings, carefully chosen and arranged to perfection.

These are but a few of scores of instances. They cannot be explained in any other way. They have been revealed by God and transmit divine rather than human knowledge. They are characterized by precision, perfect structure, and comprehensive knowledge, inimitable.

Every time you try to change the position of a word in the Qur'an, not to say replace it by another, you will be struck by the impossibility of the task. You will realize that you are facing a kind of linguistic and scientific inevitability that is truly stunning, an instance of absolute truth. Look at the following verse dealing with bribery in the second surah of the Qur'an:

> *And do not eat up your property among yourselves*
> *For vanities, nor use it as bait for the judges,*
> *With intent that ye may eat up wrongfully and knowingly*
> *A little of (other) people's property.*
> *(The Heifer, 2: 188)*

The word *bait* may sound odd because for the judge or ruler, the Arabic word, allows both meanings, and has a higher station in life than that of the plaintiff or any of the ruler's subjects; but the reason for this is obvious. Once he accepts a bribe, the ruler or judge will be lower in position than his subjects. The hand that gives is the upper hand. Hence this perfect metaphoric expression is impossible to replace, and no other term can, in fact, be more precise and fitting.

The examples are interminable. We have unraveled the mystery of some words, but others remain mysterious. It is a Book sublime; falsehood comes not to it from before it nor from behind it. Science races breathlessly but has no chance of catching up with it. If we add to this that this Qur'an, the stunning miracle that it is, was recited by an unlettered man from the tribe of Quraish, a shepherd who tended his flocks in a desert inhabited only by Bedouins and cut off from civilization and science, we shall realize the magnitude of this real miracle. No one could dispute it unless he had an obstinate, perverse mind, and deadened feelings. He would, indeed, be a blind man intellectually and morally, having chosen to punish himself by shutting out from his spirit the warm light of mercy, kindness, and love which radiates from that sublime Book. May God show him mercy and open up his heart to His light.

> *Truly it is not their eyes that are blind,*
> *But their hearts which are in their breasts.*
> *(The Pilgrimage, 22: 46)*

THE AUTHOR

DR. MOSTAFA MAHMOUD was born in Egypt on December 27, 1931 and received his medical degree from Cairo University in 1952. A physician by training, he read avidly, roaming at will from anatomy to astronomy, from biology to zoogeography. After working as a physician for a few years he turned his full talents to his favorite hobby – literary writing, where he started as a liberal intellectual. His weekly articles, *Midnight Journals*, on science and philosophy, attracted large sections of the reading public in the Arab world. His articles reflected the variety of the points of view adopted and the open mind with which he approached all questions of science and human thought. As a successful author who churned out novel after novel, play after play, he relished the controversies that most of them aroused. He has authored over ninety books on a variety of topics many of which have been translated into several languages.

He is also the Founder and Chairman of the Board of Mahmoud Mosque Society, the largest charity organization in Egypt. Today, this Society runs its mosque and four specialized hospitals in Cairo, maintains a museum of geology and astronomy, provides social support to 4,000 families, and manages a food bank that helps thousands of needy family in various neighborhoods of greater Cairo metropolitan area.

THE TRANSLATOR

DR. M. M. ENANI is a playwright, critic and a distinguished translator who has published a number of English translations for famous Egyptian writers and poets. He is Professor of literature at the University of Cairo.